DBT WORKBOOK

FOR TEENS AND PARENTS

(2 BOOKS IN 1)

Effective Dialectical Behavior Therapy Skills for
Adolescents to Manage Anger, Anxiety, and
Intense Emotions

The Mentor Bucket

TABLE OF CONTENTS

Book – 1: The DBT Skills Workbook for Teens

Book – 2: DBT Skills Workbook for Parents of Teens

BOOK - 1

THE DBT SKILLS
WORKBOOK FOR TEENS

Understand Your Emotions and
Manage Anxiety, Anger,
and Other Negativity to Balance Your Life for
The Better

The Mentor Bucket

INTRODUCTION

There is no denying it—life has given you countless reasons to feel scared, angry, sad, and frustrated. Sometimes, the feeling may seem okay. Other times, it feels as if your emotions have taken you over, and they spiral out of control as if they've got a mind of their own. To make things worse, the consuming emotions start interfering with your studies, causing you trouble when you try to make friends or preventing you from achieving your goals and enjoying your teen years.

If your teenage years seem stressful because you can't balance school and homework with your social and family life, you are likely walking through an array of emotions. Perhaps, you easily get frustrated and upset because someone in your school is spreading lies about you, or you feel very anxious because you are under some sort of pressure to outshine everyone else to secure your future. The truth is, you can't keep living like this. You can't keep struggling when you are supposed to be enjoying your teenage years and starting to follow those dreams you have.

Of course, there has to be a way to handle the roller coaster of emotions you are experiencing, and your reading this book shows that you've been seeking answers. Luckily, you are in the right place.

If you are ready to take charge of your emotions, achieve your goals, and be the best version of yourself, you can apply Dialectical Behavioral Therapy (DBT) skills. These can help you understand and manage your fluctuating emotions, improve your self-awareness, overcome impulsive behaviors, and effectively deal with relationship issues.

As a teen, you are naturally programmed to seek added information from outside your familial nucleus and to enjoy receiving attention from your peers. During these years, your learning ability has changed from concrete to abstract. You've experienced a change that involves identifying as a separate individual from your family or parents and facing an emotional separation from them. You see yourself as an individual with a sexual identity, and you now identify with your peers and have the drive to learn and explore the world. Additionally, your bio-sexual development is now slowly kicking into full gear; you are beginning to feel your emotions as much stronger than ever.

As a result, you may start struggling with managing and regulating your emotions, impulses, feelings, and relationships. When you struggle to manage these aspects, you may start experiencing additional issues such as anxiety, trauma, self-esteem, and poor grades, among other things.

These days, parents are more focused on teaching their children about hygiene, safety, and expected performance in school. They find themselves neglecting to teach physiological and emotional self-care. Teenagers are often not provided with enough guidance and information on how to handle their emotions, physical wellbeing, and relationships. However, in this fast-paced, ever-changing world, teenagers need to learn more about their emotions and how to be in control.

DBT is an evidence-based therapy that aims to teach individuals how to manage their emotions and thoughts and to build healthier relationships. Using DBT involves learning how to use its skills, including emotional regulation, mindfulness, interpersonal effectiveness, and distress tolerance.

The DBT-supported skills are important for all teens to learn, whether they've been diagnosed with a mental illness or need an effective way to manage their emotions, including anxiety, stress, anger, and sadness. DBT will increase your self-awareness and equip you with the tools to master managing your emotions and building healthier relationships.

For many years now, DBT has helped teenagers and adults struggle with frequent mood swings, angry outbursts, impulsive/disruptive behaviors, anxiety and depression, alcohol and drug abuse, suicidal behaviors, poor coping skills, family/peer conflict, and eating disorder behaviors.

While some people are better at managing their emotions than others, DBT can come through for those who seem to always find emotional balance impossible. DBT can avail you of the skills needed to handle your emotions and the feelings you experience while going through the difficult stage that takes you into adulthood. When your emotions are managed properly, you will have the interpersonal tools to build healthier relationships and effectively manage your behaviors and actions.

This book is for teenagers who intend to learn skills to help them manage their emotions as well as for parents who want to understand what their teens learn and how to help them.

For over twenty years now, DBT has become widely known and practiced by clinicians to help patients struggling to achieve mental wellness. It is a model of therapy that was first created to help chronically injurious behaviors and the suicidal population. As a result of this approach, DBT is now an effective method to cure a variety of mental health conditions.

I first learned about DBT when working as a clinician and helping the populace in battling persistent and severe mental illness. For every ten clients I talked to, seven were battling mental health conditions that included anxiety, depression, anger, trauma, suicide, and Post Traumatic Stress Disorder.

Fortunately, I had just received my DBT training and could attend to them and serve their needs. For many years now, after learning all about DBT, I've been helping people by utilizing DBT skills for teenagers especially.

I want this workbook to serve as a means of reaching a wider audience because I know many people are experiencing emotional challenges and want to set themselves free from the shackles of a roller coaster of emotions.

This workbook has been written in an easy format for your understanding. It is divided into six chapters, with worksheets and exercises you'll want to work engage with. The workbook extensively discusses what DBT is, how it can help you, and how to use DBT skills to overcome emotional issues such as anger, anxiety, trauma, and Post-Traumatic Stress Disorder (PTSD).

We'll start this book by explaining all you need to know about DBT and why you should pay attention to this form of therapy. This will serve as a foundational chapter, whereas other ideas will be built on as we progress with the workbook.

Are you ready to start this exciting journey with me?

I think I just got a resounding YES from you! Then let's get started!

CHAPTER 1:
DBT AND HOW IT WORKS

DBT may sound strange to most people, or perhaps they've heard about it but don't know what it entails. Well, newsflash: I was once like you. When I first heard of DBT, I immediately assumed it was a complicated treatment and wasn't willing to give it a chance until much later. I hope that won't be the case for you. Regardless, I will be making sure I break it down for easier understanding.

First, I would like to answer the question, "What is dialectal?" If you've hurriedly picked up your phone to do a quick search, then I am sorry to let you know that Wikipedia and Google aren't that helpful in making you understand this word. They've defined dialectal with bogus words, making it even harder to understand what it really means.

When I ask people what dialectal means, I often hear them say "dialogue," "discussion between two people," "something related to two things," and "the way people talk, like their dialect."

Psychologist and creator of DBT, Marsha Linehan, defines dialectal as an integration of two opposites. In other words, dialectal is when two opposing things are being true all at once. It is the existence of opposites, for which people are taught two opposite strategies (acceptance and change). This implies that they will have to make positive changes to manage their emotions and forge ahead.

If that's still confusing, let me give you an instance to gain a better idea of what dialectal means.

Say you have a sister you love dearly. However, she is always busy because she is working two full-time jobs at the moment. You have a question you need to ask her, and you've been trying to reach her for days now to get the answer. Either she doesn't pick up, or she picks up and abruptly tells you that she will call you back. This has been irking you. You care about her and think she is a nice person, but her being unavailable most times is something you don't like about her. Well, this is actually a dialectal situation.

There are two opposing facts about how you feel about your sister, and they are true at the same time.

This brings us to the term Dialectal Behavioral Therapy (DBT). What really is it? What does it entail?

What Is DBT?

DBT is a cognitive behavioral treatment. While Cognitive Behavioral Therapy (CBT) aims to identify and change your negative thinking patterns through positive behavioral changes, DBT provides you with new skills for managing your discomforting and painful emotions, while at the same time reducing the conflict you may be having in relationships. The main goal of DBT is to teach you to live in the moment and have healthier ways of coping with stress, regulating your emotions, and improving your relationships.

Originally, DBT was developed for treating chronically suicidal individuals diagnosed with Borderline Personality Disorder (BPD). Currently, it has gained the attention of the populace and is now the gold standard of psychological treatments for people with different mental health conditions.

DBT effectively treats people who have difficulty regulating their emotions or people showing self-destructive behaviors such as substance abuse and eating disorders. Also, it can be used to treat trauma and post-traumatic stress disorder (PTSD).

DBT equips you with new skills to manage your emotions. It focuses on providing you with therapeutic skills in four key areas. The first is mindfulness, which focuses on improving your ability to accept and be in the present. The second is distress tolerance, and this aims at increasing your tolerance for negative emotions instead of avoiding them.

The third is emotional regulation, which entails providing you with strategies needed to manage and change the intense emotions that are causing you distress. And the last is interpersonal effectiveness, which entails techniques that allow you to communicate more assertively, command self-respect, and improve your relationships. I will be explaining more about the skills of DBT shortly.

Conditions That DBT Treats

DBT has been endorsed by the American Psychiatric Association (APA) as an effective treatment in treating BPD. Teens who utilized DBT have been reported as seeing improvements such as less anger, improved social functioning, less likelihood of relapse, less severe suicidal behavior, and more confidence in handling emotions.

Studies have revealed DBT to be an effective therapy that helps teens suffering from anxiety, depression, and trauma. Your healthcare provider or therapist may suggest DBT be used on its own or in combination with medications.

Conditions that DBT effectively treats include:

Borderline Personality Disorder

DBT has its history with borderline personality disorder (BPD); this was the first condition it was used to treat. BPD is a condition affecting how one feels about themselves. Having intense emotions and unstable relationships with others are characteristics of BPD. According to research, DBT can be used to manage these symptoms (Chapman, 2006).

Suicidal Thoughts

Dr. Marsha Linehan first discovered the connection between suicidal thoughts and BPD. She realized that using DBT to treat people with BPD significantly reduced the risk of attempting suicide, a key marker for people with BPD.

This totally makes sense because people who have suicidal thoughts also find it hard to manage their intense emotions, tolerate their distress, and communicate with people. DBT can effectively address these symptoms and help individuals develop useful coping strategies.

Self-Harm

Deliberately harming yourself can happen on its own or be due to another mental health condition. Individuals who attempt to harm themselves do so as a way to escape a painful experience or difficult feelings.

With DBT, they can learn better ways to cope with these painful emotions, urges, and memories. With DBT, the individual will learn to accept these feelings as part of their experience, form a tolerance for distress, and better regulate their emotions.

Eating Disorders

While CBT is highly effective in helping people with eating disorders, it is not suitable for everyone. Research has suggested DBT as an alternate treatment that may be beneficial in some types of these cases.

People with eating disorders usually engage in unhealthy habits to escape, manage, and control their intense emotions. Since this is the case for many people, DBT can teach the individual other, healthier methods for coping with these emotions. This type of therapy works best for individuals with a binge eating disorder or bulimia nervosa and is not too helpful for individuals with anorexia nervosa.

Depression

DBT wasn't created to treat depression. However, due to its core premise, it has been found to be effective in treating the condition. The therapy emphasizes tolerance and validation, which are both in short supply for people with depression. People with depression normally feel worthless, which creates an overwhelming sense of sadness and invalidates almost all aspects of their lives.

With DBT, they will be equipped with coping mechanisms that allow them to address the negative aspects of their lives and break free from depression. This process may take time, but it's highly effective in the long term.

Benefits and Effectiveness

Many studies have suggested that DBT effectively treats borderline personality disorder, proving its benefits. The founder of this therapy conducted most of the studies herself and discovered these benefits.

DBT focuses on validating your experience and encouraging you to love and accept yourself while pushing for self-improvement. This approach to mental wellness is what gives you the skills you need for the following:

Improving Your Relationships

When dealing with any mental health condition, it's always beneficial to have a good support network. Many other therapies have failed to take this into consideration, and they expect you to do it alone. With DBT, there is an advocacy for understanding the role social relationship plays in overcoming the challenges that follow a mental illness.

When you create healthy relationships with trustworthy and respectful boundaries, you will experience improved health and general wellbeing in different ways.

Going Beyond Mental Illness

Even though the initial aim of DBT is to reduce the symptoms in people experiencing mental illness, it can go beyond that. The skills of DBT can now be applied to other areas of life as well.

For example, research has revealed that mindfulness is helpful in wellbeing and other aspects of life. With this skill, you can experience an improved aspect of your home, work, and play.

Improving Your Quality of Life

One of the main objectives of DBT is to improve one's quality of life. Sometimes, we aren't in control of what happens to us, and we can't foresee the future. Some people will experience mental health challenges as an everlasting part of their lives, and accepting this as a fact is important in moving forward.

DBT can help these individuals by improving the quality of their lives—encouraging them to make changes and go in the right direction while letting them know that it's okay to experience difficulties. People experiencing disruptive and intense emotions can have their quality of life severely impacted.

Managing Stress

The features of DBT support you in building the skills that will help you manage stress and stressors. Many people struggling with self-harm, suicide, and risky behavior engage in these because they are stressed and can't manage their mental illness in better ways. With DBT, patients will accept their stressors and manage them with positive coping mechanisms.

Controlling Destructive Thoughts or Actions

When using the skills of DBT, you will likely analyze your behavioral patterns and thoughts, take note of the destructive ones, and replace them with positive and healthy ones. If you find it difficult to regulate your emotions, learning to control and replace them is a significant part of living a healthier and happy life.

Improving Self-Perception

DBT encourages recognizing strengths and improving weaknesses. With a combined effort of positive support and self-improvement, you can counter the negative self-perception that usually accompanies a mental health condition.

Finally, as you focus on facts rather than your emotions or judgments, DBT will help you improve your ability to respond positively and productively without engaging in destructive thoughts, behaviors, and self-blame.

DBT Skills

DBT comprises four core skills that are called the modules. These skills help you cope with emotional distress positively and productively. According to Linehan, the four skills are the *"active ingredients"* of DBT.

Here is what the four skills entail:

Mindfulness

This skill is about having awareness and accepting what's happening in your present moment. With mindfulness, you can learn to notice and accept your feelings and thoughts without judgment.

Mindfulness is broken down into *"what"* skills and *"how"* skills when used in the context of DBT.

The *"what"* skills aim to teach you what you should focus on. They can be:

- Your present
- Your thoughts, emotions, and sensations
- Your awareness in the present
- The separation of your sensations and emotions from your thoughts

The *"how"* skills teach you to be more mindful through the following:

- Taking effective actions
- Balancing your emotions with rational thoughts
- Using mindfulness skills regularly
- Learning and tolerating aspects of yourself through radical acceptance
- Overcoming the things that are hindering mindfulness. For example, doubt, sleepiness, and restlessness

Emotion Regulation

You may feel like you can't escape your emotions, and this makes you feel helpless. But with a little help, it's possible to manage your emotions no matter how overwhelming they feel.

Emotion regulation skills can help you learn how to deal with the primary emotional reactions that tend to lead you toward distressing secondary reactions. For instance, a primary emotion of anger may lead to feelings of shame, guilt, worthlessness, and depression.

With emotion regulation skills, you can learn to:

- Reduce vulnerability
- Identify emotions
- Solve problems in helpful ways
- Increase emotions that have positive effects
- Overcome barriers to emotions that have positive effects
- Expose yourself to your emotions
- Become mindful of your emotions without judgment
- Not give in to emotional urges

Distress Tolerance

Even though mindfulness is very effective, it isn't always enough, especially when you are experiencing a crisis. This is where distress tolerance proves very helpful. With DBT skills, you can get through challenging times without using destructive coping mechanisms.

During a crisis, you may apply certain coping mechanisms to deal with the emotions that come with the crisis. For example, avoidance or self-isolation won't help you, even if they give temporary relief. Other coping mechanisms such as an angry outburst, self-harm, and substance abuse will cause harm instead.

With distress tolerance skills, you can:

- Soothe yourself by relaxing and using your sense of feeling at peace
- Distract yourself until you feel calm enough to deal with the emotion or situation
- Compare coping strategies by listing their advantages and disadvantages
- Devise means to improve the moment despite the difficulty

Interpersonal Effectiveness

When you feel intense emotions and rapid mood swings, it makes it difficult for you to relate with others. Knowing what you want and how you feel is an integral part of building helpful connections. With interpersonal effectiveness, you can become clearer about the effects of your feelings.

Interpersonal effectiveness combines social skills, listening skills, and assertiveness training to teach you how to change the situation while staying true to your values.

The skills include:

- Building respect for yourself (self-respect effectiveness)
- Learning the right way to ask for what you want and then taking the right steps to get it (objective effectiveness)
- Learning to walk through conflicts in relationships (interpersonal effectiveness)

DBT Techniques

DBT utilizes three main approaches to teach the core skills we just discussed. It is believed that the combination of these techniques is what makes DBT effective.

The techniques are:

Skills Training

The skills training group is similar to a group therapy session. These groups last for 24 weeks and meet once a week for two or three hours. Despite this, some DBT programs repeat the skills training to design them to last for a year.

In the skills group, you will learn and practice each skill and talk through scenarios with others in the group.

One-On-One Therapy

DBT usually requires one hour of one-on-one therapy every week. During these sessions, you get to talk with your therapist about your feelings, what you are dealing with, and what you are trying to manage. Your therapist will also use this time to build your skills and help you by navigating your challenges.

Phone Coaching

Phone coaching is also a technique some therapists use to provide extra support between your one-on-one appointments. If you often need extra support because you usually feel overwhelmed, phone coaching can be very helpful. Your therapist will guide you on how to use DBT skills to overcome your current challenges.

CHAPTER 2:
UNDERSTANDING YOUR EMOTIONS

In the previous chapter, we discussed DBT and how it works. This chapter will take things a step further by discussing emotions and making intense emotions more bearable with different exercises. When your emotions are less intense, they become easier to manage; this helps get you off the emotional roller coaster when you find yourself on one.

Naming Your Emotions

The first step in understanding your emotions is naming them. How do you describe your emotional state? Do you normally use words such as "upset" or "bad" to describe how you feel? The truth is, these words are generic and don't faithfully describe your emotional state. When you say you are "upset," what does that mean? Does it mean you are sad? Angry? Or anxious? Being upset can mean any of these, so it's important to be specific about how you truly feel to enable you to know what to do about the emotion.

So, how do you name your emotion? Let's quickly look at the exercises below.

Exercise: Naming Emotions

Many words can be used to describe the eight basic emotions we have. However, each word comes with a slight difference in the "feel" or "flavor" of the emotion. It's better to have more words for the emotions you feel to help you describe your experience.

Below are eight primary emotions with a list of possible words that match them. Write the primary emotion that best matches the possible words listed in the space provided.

The Primary Emotions are Anger, Fear, Surprise, Interest, Joy, Sorrow, Disgust, and Shame.

The list of possible words:

Alarmed:

Nervous:

Hot-headed:

Depressed: ....

Ecstatic: ....

Up-tight: ....

Joyous: ....

Revolted: ....

Hot-headed: ....

Infuriated: ....

Sorrowful: ....

Miserable: ....

Annoyed: ....

Down in the dumps: ....

Livid: ....

Giddy: ....

Grossed-out: ....

In despair: ....

Afraid: ....

Restless: ....

Jubilant: ....

Exercise: Naming your emotions worksheet

A time I felt angry was when:

_____

_____

_____

_____

A time I felt nervous was when:

_____

_____

_____

A time I felt afraid was when:

A time I felt depressed was when:

A time I felt joyous was when:

A time I felt confused was when:

A time I felt disappointed was when:

27

The Role of Emotions (Information, Communication, and Motivation)

After naming your emotions, what next? This section will discuss changing how you think about your emotions. This will be done by looking at their role or the function they serve.

You might not be aware of this, but emotions have essential functions and are needed even though they sometimes feel uncomfortable. While you might just want to toss them away, emotions are still needed and can't be tossed aside. This is why it's important to know their functions and learn to accept them.

According to the workings of DBT, there are three main reasons you experience emotions: information, communication, and motivation. Let's quickly discuss these reasons below.

Information

Your emotions are there to provide you with the information you need, though they can be modified to ensure they're more suited to your requirements. For example, the emotion "anger" can make you aware that something is wrong with a situation you see as unfair already or one you don't like for a certain reason. The emotions "shame" and "guilt" may arise to make you realize that you are engaging in something that's against your values and morals.

DBT has taught us that our emotions communicate with us by giving us emotional information before the brain can process the information received from our senses.

For example, you are walking home with your friends, and you decide to take the park route. You take the lead, and when you look ahead, you see something dark and shiny coiled up on the side of the path you are supposed to take. Immediately, fear kicks in to stop you from taking a step further and to keep you safe from what seems like a poisonous snake. This is done before your brain even has the chance to process the scene.

Have you ever been in a situation where your emotions fed you with information that made you see that you needed to act in a certain way, but they made things different than how you would have liked? Perhaps there was a time when your emotions gave you information that made you act in a certain way without even thinking about the rationale behind it?

It all borders on your emotions serving the function of providing you with information.

Motivation

Another function of your emotion is to motivate you to act. For example, it's natural to feel angry when you get bullied. As a result, you get motivated to take action against the bullying behavior by informing your teachers or the school authorities about the situation. You can also be motivated to participate in school campaigns to increase awareness of bullying and how to prevent it. Without the emotion "anger" to fuel your actions, there is every possibility that nothing will be done to improve the situation.

Another emotion that can motivate you is "fear." Immediately as your brain senses something that is a threat, you enter a fight or flight mode that triggers you to either run away from the situation or to stand and fight. Whatever your action may be, your emotion motivates you to act.

For example, you've just left your friend's place. You're walking home, and it's almost dark because you had to stay late to work on a group assignment together. You hear a strange noise, and immediately your fight-or-flight response kicks in. All your senses become heightened as you're trying to figure out what the strange noise is all about and whether it's a sign of danger. Your heart starts beating quickly, and your muscles tense. Then you see a strange man walking toward you, and I guess your next action will be to run back to your friend's house to ensure your safety. Your motivation for taking that action was triggered by fear, and that's what will get you to safety.

Communication

Another role your emotions play is in helping you communicate effectively with others. Your emotions are connected to specific body language and facial expressions, making it easy to identify them in you and in others. For example, people around you can easily guess how you feel based on your facial expression and body language. You don't need to tell them that you are sad when you have teary eyes or are sobbing. You also don't need to tell them that you are angry when your fist is clenched and your face is red. By looking at your expressions, they can guess how you feel and try to help you.

Can you remember any situation where your emotion served the role of communication for you? Maybe you felt sad, but even without your mentioning it, a friend tried talking to you to cheer you up. Or perhaps you wanted to scold your younger sibling for doing something wrong, but because of the emotion they expressed, you changed your mind and consoled them instead.

It's important to know that even though your emotions exist to serve a purpose, they aren't foolproof and shouldn't be treated as authoritative. Feeling a certain way about something doesn't make it entirely true. You need to evaluate the situation and check for facts before assuming it to be true. For example, if a meal smells good, that doesn't mean it must taste good. First, before you can conclude, you need to engage your sense of taste to know if the food truly tastes good.

Your emotions are like the senses that provide your body with information. However, you need to be careful to avoid having them lead you astray. For example, seeing a stranger walking toward you and feeling threatened doesn't mean that person intends to hurt you. Because you saw a shiny black thing in your path doesn't mean it is a snake or something harmful. We'll be discussing how to reclaim your emotions in the next chapter; in the meantime, know that your emotions serve a purpose even if they don't always do it perfectly.

Exercise: Checking the Facts

When you experience some emotion, e.g., anger, it can be easy to place too much importance on the emotion and blow things out of proportion. In this Checking the Facts exercise, you can discover whether you are blowing things out of proportion and also reduce the intensity of the emotion you experience.

To check the facts, ask yourself the following questions:

What is the event that has triggered this emotion?

_____

_____

_____

_____

_____

What assumptions or interpretations am I currently making out of the event?

_____

_____

_____

_____

_____

Do my emotions and the level of their intensity correlate with the facts of the situation or my assumptions of the situation?

_____

The Connection Between Emotion, Thought, and Behavior

Emotion is a full-system response that can make a situation confusing; there will be a lot going on simultaneously with emotions. While you are feeling a certain emotion, you are also thinking certain thoughts that are triggered by the emotion, and as a result, you engage in behaviors that relate to the emotions you feel. Because of what I just described, people usually confuse their emotions with behaviors and thoughts.

There is a connection between your emotions, thoughts, and behavior; hence, the confusion. Changing your thoughts will affect your emotions and behaviors; likewise, changing your behavior will affect your thoughts and emotions. This is because the three areas are interrelated. Most times, if you are asked how you feel, the description you give usually ends up being your thoughts instead. For example, what would your response be if asked how you felt after realizing that a stranger was walking toward you? Your answer can be, "I just wanted to run as fast as my legs could take me" or "I wanted to get out of there fast." These explanations are your thoughts, and the emotions connected with these thoughts might be "fear," "anxiety," or "distrust."

The full-system response of our emotions usually happens automatically and very quickly, so we don't pause to process what is really happening before we act. Let's think about it from a different angle. Don't you think acting without pausing to think clearly is one of the reasons our emotions get us into trouble? For this reason, it is important to learn how to separate emotions from behaviors and thoughts.

The naming of the emotions exercise you engaged in earlier will help you separate your emotions from your thoughts and behaviors. Right now, it's left for you to figure out what exactly you are feeling versus what you are thinking and how you are behaving.

Let's use our earlier examples to break this down and give you a clearer picture.

It's getting dark, and you are walking home from your friend's place alone. You suddenly hear a strange noise. Your experience might be something like this: Oh! What was that (your thought)? You look around, trying to assess the scenario (your behavior), and you notice that you don't recognize any familiar face. You start thinking, what if people are following me? What if I get attacked (your thoughts)? You start feeling anxious and scared (your emotions). If it is someone dangerous, would I be able to fight the person off? No one I know can help me (your thoughts). From this thinking, your fear increases (your emotion). Suddenly, you have the urge to run and escape whatever it is (your thought). You start considering what you should do (your thought). Immediately, you turn around and run back to your friend's house (your behavior).

Now, we will look at how the outcome of this scenario can change if one aspect of the experience is changed.

It's getting dark, and you are walking home from your friend's place alone. You suddenly hear a strange noise. Your initial thought might be: Oh! What was that (your thought)? You are looking around, trying to assess the scenario (your behavior), and suddenly you see people you don't recognize. You start wondering who they are because they don't look familiar (your thought). You are curious (your emotion) and continue to observe them (your thought). You notice two teenage girls standing in the corner of the park (your thought). You realize that they are looking at the street sign and their mobile phones; they may be lost (your thought). You start considering what you should do (your thought). Since it is getting dark, you are a bit concerned about the girls (your emotion). Then you approach them to ask if they are lost and need help finding the right way (your behavior).

We've just described two different outcomes based on the same beginning. Can you now notice that your behaviors and emotions can be influenced by changing your thoughts about the scenario?

Do you understand the connection now? If you don't, let's look at one more example to help you grasp it.

One afternoon, you return from school and inform your parents that you scored a "C" on your Mathematics test (your behavior). Even before telling them, you felt disappointed in yourself for having that score, and you are worried about how you will cope (your emotion). You're not sure if it will affect your chances of getting accepted in your preferred college (your thought). After informing your parents, they express the same concern, and you are upset with them immediately (your emotion), thinking they are always disappointed in you (your thought). You then yell at them and storm off to your room (your behavior).

Now, let's look at how the outcome of this scenario can change if one aspect of the experience is changed.

One afternoon, you return from school and inform your parents that you scored a "C" on your Mathematics test (your behavior). Even before telling them, you started feeling disappointed in yourself for having that score (your emotion), and you are worried about how you will cope (your emotion). You're not sure if it will affect your chances of getting accepted in your preferred college (your thought). After informing your parents, they express the same concern, and you are upset with them immediately (your emotion), thinking they are disappointed in you (your thought). You notice this thought, and instead of reacting rashly, you talk back to it. You realize they are disappointed in you because they notice you are disappointed in yourself (your thought). You then express your worry to your parents (your behavior). They give you some reassurance, which helps you change your thoughts and emotions about your Mathematics grade.

Now, don't just say that was quite easy. What I've given are just examples to demonstrate the idea of the connection between your emotions, behaviors, and thoughts. It definitely requires lots of practice to change your emotions, thoughts, and behavior. The first step is to understand why and how it is helpful to you when you do change them. Then you will start practicing the examples in this chapter. Before we come to the end of this section, quickly practice the following PLEASE exercise.

Exercise: PLEASE

The PLEASE exercise will help you acknowledge the connection between your brain and body. It becomes easier to manage your emotions when you know how to manage your body and health.

It entails remembering to:

- PL – Treat your **physical illness**
- E – **Eat** healthy meals
- A – **Avoid** mood-altering drugs
- S – **Sleep** well
- E – **Exercise**

These suggestions above should be followed to ensure your body is healthy and happy, making it easier for your mind to stay healthy and happy too.

PLEASE Worksheet

What do I need to do to ensure that my physical wellness doesn't affect my emotional wellness?

_____

_____

_____

What changes can I make to my diet to ensure I achieve emotional wellness?

_____

_____

_____

_____

_____

_____

What are the three main motivations I can use to avoid mood-altering substances?

_____

_____

What sleep issues should I discuss with the doctor?

What activities can I engage in every day to ensure I get enough physical activity for the day?

CHAPTER 3:
RECLAIMING CONTROL OF YOUR EMOTIONS

Your emotions play a significant role in how you react. When you are in tune with your emotions, you will have access to vital knowledge that helps you make your relationships a success, make effective decisions, enjoy better communication, and take good care of yourself. While your emotions play an important role in your life, they can also take a toll on your interpersonal relationships, emotional health, and your life in general. When this happens, you will start feeling that they are out of control.

According to a Tarzana therapist, Vicki Botnick, any positive or negative emotion can intensify and get to the point where it becomes difficult to control. However, by pointing it in the right direction, you can take control of the reins, which we'll discuss in this chapter.

First, let's look at how the thought process works so we can better understand how to reclaim control of intense emotions.

The Three Thought Processes

According to DBT, there are three things you apply when you do any thinking: the reasoning self, the emotional self, and the wise self. If you are riding the emotional roller coaster, you will most likely think by using your emotional self. However, other thinking perspectives are equally important for you to access the different states that will improve how you manage your emotions.

The following section will discuss each way of thinking to help you practice knowing your state of mind.

Reasoning Self

In this state of thinking, you use your logical thinking and are straightforward with your thoughts. You only consider facts and do not judge with your emotions. There are usually no emotions in the reasoning state, and if there are, they are minimal and won't affect how you act. An example of the emotional reasoning self is when you choose a college because of the courses they offer, the school's reputation, and the likelihood of getting employed shortly after graduating from there. This is instead of considering things such as whether you like the location of the campus, how close it is to home if you want to be visiting home, or if you have friends that will be attending the college.

Another example of being in your reasoning self is when you do your homework, and you aren't so frustrated that you want to throw your books away. Or when you follow your parents' instructions on how to do the dishes because they went out and will be home late.

Even though many people ought to be familiar with the emotional self, some are on the emotional roller coaster because they often disregard their values and emotions, acting outside of their reasoning and experiencing the subsequent negative consequences. This means that if you ignore what your values and emotions are telling you, you are probably not acting in your best interest, which may trigger emotional pain such as frustration, anger, and sadness.

Emotional Self

The emotional self is the one you probably already know. When you think and act from your emotional self, your actions are controlled by your emotions. When you feel angry, you tend to lash out at someone even if the reason for your anger has nothing to do with the person. Perhaps you feel anxious and want to avoid what's causing you anxiety. For example, you would rather stay at home and miss classes because you don't want to be part of the presentation scheduled to be held today.

By acting from your emotional self, you react from your emotions instead of choosing how you act. It will feel like your emotions are in control of you while you are just along for the ride. When in an emotional state, you're likely to do things you will regret later by acting impulsively in ways that usually come with negative consequences over time. For example, breaking up with your boyfriend/girlfriend because you got angry with them, skipping classes even when you need to get good grades, or getting drunk at a party when you are supposed to be preparing for your exams. These scenarios should sound familiar to you if you've been on an emotional roller coaster. Thankfully, it isn't static; there are things you can do to change your thinking style.

Wise Self

Engaging the wise self is when you balance your reasoning self and your emotional self. This is in between the two; you aren't choosing one or the other. With your wise self, you will consider both your reasoning and emotions while factoring in a third element—your intuition. When in a situation where your feelings creep in, you allow yourself to feel them and consider what your logic is saying about that. Then you listen to the little voice inside you weighing both the positives and negatives of the situation, which will eventually tell you what will be effective in the long term.

Can you recall a moment in your life when your wise self was screaming for your attention? Even when you don't listen to it, know it is somewhere inside you. It is important to know that what your inner wisdom signals you to do may not be easy, and it won't be what you want to do. However, it is what's best for the situation, for you, and for others around you.

Getting a Wise Self

Like with learning anything new, accessing your wise self may take lots of energy, time, and practice, especially if you are used to listening to your emotional or reasoning self. However, don't let this discourage you from trying. Like I mentioned earlier, even though it may prove difficult, it is accessible; at the end of the day, attaining the skill will be worth the effort you've invested in it. It is a skill that will bring calm and peace to your life, and this will help you survive the emotional roller coaster you will experience. As you continue practicing the skill, it will become more natural.

It is time to engage in exercises that will get you to your wise self!

Exercise: Opposite Action

The opposite action is a technique you can use to stop highly charged emotions and make them less intense. Your emotional responses are usually followed by specific behaviors, such as withdrawing from people after feeling sad, or engaging in intense arguments after getting angry.

We often assume that the connection starts from the emotion and ends in the behavior, not the other way around. The truth is, it is possible to invoke a certain emotion if you engage in behavior associated with that emotion. The logic here is that instead of engaging in what you normally do when you feel a certain way, why not do the opposite action? For example, if you feel sad, why not insert yourself into the midst of your friends and chat with them instead of withdrawing from them? When you get angry, why not talk quietly instead of yelling?

For guilt or shame:

When you feel guilty or ashamed, instead of withdrawing and avoiding the situation, why not repair the transgression by apologizing telling the person you've offended that you are sorry, making things better (doing something nice for the person), accepting the consequences of your action, ensuring you avoid making that mistake, moving on, and letting go of the emotions you feel?

For fear:

Rather than giving in and showing that you are scared, why not do the thing you are afraid of instead? Engage in activities and tasks, or go to events and places, that normally make you uncomfortable. Talk to people you are usually afraid of. Do things that will give you a sense of control and mastery over the situation. When you feel overwhelmed, break the tasks into smaller, more manageable steps.

For anger:

Rather than attacking the person you are angry with, avoid them and avoid thinking about them. Do not dwell on them, be nice to them rather than mean, and imagine showing them empathy and sympathy instead of blaming them.

For depression and sadness:

Don't avoid; be active! Engage in things that will make you feel confident and competent.

Opposite Action Worksheet

In the worksheet below, aim to follow the instructions written under the step section, which signifies what you should do. For example, under "Identify the feeling," your identified feeling can be anger as a result of feeling cheated, anxiety about spending time with others, or sadness when you are not listened to.

Then, as suggested in the examples above, do the opposite action of what comes to mind. When you feel anxious about spending time with others and you want to avoid them, face your fears instead by spending time with them. When you feel scared of doing certain tasks, get used to your fears by doing those tasks rather than avoiding them.

Step: Identify the feeling

Example: Anxiety about spending time with people and making friends

Your Turn:

For Example: I will make new friends and spend time with people rather than avoid them.

Step: Identify the resulting action

> *Example: You would rather be alone and bury yourself in work, convincing yourself that you don't have the time to make friends.*

> *Your Turn:*

Step: Do the opposite action

> *Example: Push yourself to mingle with people and attend gatherings.*

> *Your Turn:*

Step: Feel the opposite feeling

> *Example: Excitement about making new friends Relief because there won't be a "push-and-pull" about whether making friends is a good idea or not*

> *Your Turn:*

Exercise: Increasing Self-Awareness

The first area you should work on when making any change is your self-awareness. You need to be aware of your thinking style, and once you have an awareness of this, you can choose what to do about it. So, how can you have this awareness? *By Observing, Noticing,* and *Acknowledging.*

To do this, you don't need to write down what you observe and notice, but if you *can* write it down, that could be helpful. The idea is to bring awareness to your experiences as much as possible. Ask yourself, *What thinking style am I using at the moment? Am I really listening to my wise self? What is my wise self-telling me to do right now?* Do this repeatedly throughout the day. Notice what is happening inside you when you question yourself without any judgment and are just being mindful of the experience.

Self-Reflection Worksheet

It's important that you reflect on yourself when practicing healthy and productive behaviors. This way, you can know what you do well and the areas that need to be worked on. The following worksheet should be used to track your progress in encouraging healthier behaviors.

The situation that triggered the behavior

Are you happy with the behavior?

If you are not happy, what could you have done better? If you are happy, what's the positive result of the behavior?

What areas will you be mindful of to improve your behavior next time?

Exercise: Monitor your inner voice

Do you know that the words you use every day significantly impact your relationship with yourself and other people and things? Talking to yourself is one of the most natural yet underestimated skills you possess. It helps by increasing your motivation, stimulating self-reflection, and connecting you to your emotions. According to a study by Canadian professor Alain Morin, there is a pronounced connection between talking to oneself frequently and having a strong sense of self-awareness.

The quality of your inner speech is important; therefore, the more positive words you use, the better your sense of awareness becomes. Pay attention to your inner voice and how you respond to your failures and successes. The feedback loops your inner voice creates can be turned into a positive or negative experience, and since the way you talk to yourself is how you get to love yourself, it is crucial to be careful with your words.

Also, limit using words such as *"I can't,"* as that can create a negative attitude and limit your potential. It makes you doubt your potential or see a task as a burden.

Validating Your Emotions

Validating your emotions simply means being non-judgmental with your emotions. It entails accepting whatever emotion you experience. You don't need to like it, just be non-judgmental about having it and toward the emotion itself.

When you validate your emotions, you prevent the emotion from escalating and the control from getting away from you. This doesn't mean you are getting rid of the emotion — DBT's goal is against this. However, the aim is to reduce the intensity of your emotion to enable you to manage your emotions.

A very effective way to validate your emotions is by being aware of your judgment toward them. This is where the practice of mindfulness comes in, and we will be discussing more on that in the next chapter.

For now, let's focus on how you can stop judgments and accept your emotional experience in the following three ways:

Allow your emotions

Allow your emotions because by doing that, you are giving yourself permission to feel everything about the feeling you have. Instead of saying, *"I feel scared,"* the self-talk will be *"It's okay to feel scared."* I need to make this clear — I am not encouraging you to like the feeling and I'm not saying that you shouldn't make an effort to change the feeling. You need to acknowledge that you have normal human emotions, and it is okay for people to feel that way. It doesn't mean you are a bad person, and neither is it the end of the world.

Acknowledge your emotions

The next technique is to acknowledge the experience. By naming or labeling your emotion, you validate it without judging it. This may seem basic or simple, but it is very effective.

Understand your emotions

You can validate your emotion by being aware of the emotional context. When you understand why you feel the way you feel in a certain moment, your emotion makes more sense. You may not always know where your emotions come from. However, remember not to judge yourself for whatever you feel.

The following mindfulness exercise will help change your attitude toward your emotions and yourself so you will validate your emotions in the long run.

Exercise: Loving-Kindness Meditation

The Loving Kindness Meditation (LKM) was formerly known as Metta Bhavana in the Pali language. Metta means kindness, love, and friendliness, while Bhavana means the act of cultivating. This simple mindfulness practice is done in five stages and should last for approximately five minutes.

Here is how to do it:

Stage 1: Feel the Metta (love) you have for yourself by being aware; focusing on peace, calm, and tranquility. Say out loud, *"May I be happy and at peace,"* and *"May I do well and be fulfilled."* Repeat these to stimulate the Metta in you.

Stage 2: Think of a good friend of yours. Remember their good qualities, feel the affinity you have for them (the connection you have with them) and encourage the feelings to increase by saying, *"May they be happy,"* and *"May they be at peace."* Picture an image of a shining light (halo) moving from your heart to theirs.

Stage 3: Think of someone you know but feel indifferent about. You neither like nor hate them, but you feel neutral toward them. Reflect on their humanity and add them to your feelings of Metta.

Stage 4: Think of someone you dislike or hate — perhaps a personal enemy. As you think of them, avoid getting caught up in the feelings of having hatred for them. Instead, think of them in a positive light and send them Metta.

Stage 5: Think of all four people altogether — yourself, your friend, the person you feel indifferent about, and the person you don't like. Start extending the feeling to everyone around you, your neighborhood, city, state, country, and all of the world. Slowly relax and bring the meditation to an end.

By doing this loving-kindness meditation, you are developing a positive wave that spreads to everyone and everywhere from your heart.

Explain how you felt when you connected with your body and focused on your breathing? Write down the feelings you had.

What distractions popped in during the exercise? Any common themes with your thoughts?

Who did you recall that made you happy and have deep feel-ings for?

What feelings did you notice in your body when thinking about the person?

Who came to your mind when thinking of someone you didn't like? How does thinking about them make you feel?

What sensations and feelings did you notice after thinking of this person in a positive light?

What sensations and feelings did you notice when extending love to everyone?

Maintaining Emotional Balance

This is a way of maintaining balance in your life. You don't want to remain in your reasoning self, and you don't want to remain in your emotional self, although both states are helpful and needed sometimes. For example, your emotional self-comprises pleasurable emotions such as joy, love, and excitement, so you wouldn't want to miss out on these emotions even when they are intense. Also, you will need your reasoning self to help you think logically about things. In all of this, the goal is to access your wisdom as much as needed, balance your emotions with your reasoning, and use your intuition to make healthier and wiser decisions.

This should be something we do daily, not just when we have life-changing decisions to make. It could be something as simple as the decision you make to go to school early to have enough time to prepare for your exams.

There are times when you act out of your wise self, but you don't get to notice it. It's time you start really seeing it so that you can appreciate yourself when you use it. Note, it is equally important that you are aware when you're acting from your reasoning or emotional self because when you are in this state and aware that you are, you will have the option to move to your wise self.

Lifestyle Changes for Emotional Balance

For many years now, research has revealed the connection between the mind and the body, knowing that how we treat our bodies greatly affects our minds and the other way around. The following section will discuss healthier choices you need to make to better control your emotions, and making these choices will improve your ability to slow down the emotional roller coaster.

Balance your sleep

Sleep is important for restoring your optimal daily functioning, and a lack of it can make you sensitive and emotionally aroused to stressful situations. Good sleep is key in your ability to cope with the emotional instability you experience in your daily life. While proper sleep helps regulate your emotions, lack of it can be detrimental to your emotional health and cause distress.

Aim to have at least eight to ten hours of sleep daily for effective emotional functioning. Getting an adequate amount of sleep helps promote improved health and mood.

Reduce caffeine and other stimulants

Many people rely on caffeine and other stimulants to keep themselves awake and energized. But do you know that caffeine and other stimulants can negatively affect your sleep and cause emotional instability? Caffeine can stay in your system for as long as 14 hours, so when you consume it in the middle of the day, that can affect your sleep later and make you feel uneasy.

Since we are all different, things may affect us differently. I want you to conduct an experiment for two weeks. Avoid taking caffeine and other stimulants during this time, and then pay attention to how you feel after the experiment. Do you feel better or worse? If you have improved sleep, that's a sign for you to reduce your caffeine intake.

Balance your nutrition

People's popular idea about balanced nutrition is that it is crucial only for optimal physical health. But do you know that eating a balanced meal also plays a crucial role in stabilizing your emotions? What you eat plays a role in hormonal balance and good mental health. To achieve emotional balance, ensure you improve your nutrition. Include a sensible proportion of proteins, carbohydrates, fats, and other beneficial nutrients in your meals. Also, stay hydrated by drinking enough fluids.

Start exercising

There are so many reasons for you to start exercising, including keeping you healthy and maintaining a healthy weight. However, it goes beyond that; exercising benefits your emotional health. It is a powerful drug without side effects (unless you have an adverse medical condition).

Engage in physical activities such as biking, walking, yoga, dancing, and Tai chi. Engaging in these exercises regularly will help improve your sleep, enhance your mood, increase your energy level, and reduce stress and feelings of depression. So, the next time you notice yourself feeling angry, stressed, and anxious, that may be a sign for you to start moving.

CHAPTER 4:
MINDFUL LIVING

How often do you find yourself distracted from thinking about your present moment? You are most likely to be distracted by thinking about everything but the present. Maybe you are working on a project, and instead of focusing on it, you are thinking about the football game you've planned with your friends for the weekend, the fight you had with your best friend, or what you will buy for your girlfriend for Valentine's Day. Perhaps, you are slightly thinking about what you are currently doing, but without your full attention. Does this sound familiar? I am guessing it does.

When you are mindful, you bring your attention back to what you are doing in the present. Being mindful is when you are working on a project, and your attention wanders to the football game you have with your friends for the weekend — you notice that your mind has wandered, so you carefully guide your attention back to the present. When your mind wanders, you notice it and do your best to bring your attention to what you are doing at that moment. This chapter will focus on the importance of mindful living and how you can use the act of mindfulness to control intense emotions and be in charge of what you feel.

Practicing Mindfulness

Mindfulness is a core DBT skill that wakes you up to life. Before you can change something, you need to wake up to it and be aware of it, and that is what mindfulness stands for. You need to be aware of your reality, your reaction, your influence over others, and what's happening around you.

When you are mindful, you are doing one thing at a time and doing it with your full attention and acceptance. You will realize that the world isn't passing you by anymore as you become more aware of your self, emotions, feelings, thoughts, and the physical sensations in your body. You will become more aware of what's going on in your surroundings and can get involved in it.

Leaving the Judgments Out

Many of us aren't aware that our words can negatively affect our emotions. When we judge, we are intensifying the emotions we experience. Think about it—have you ever been so frustrated, angry, and annoyed about something that you vent to someone about it? You may start saying things like, "Why would he say such stupid things to me?" or "That was so ridiculous of him to do that."

Think about the judgments you've made here (i.e., stupid and ridiculous). What have they done to your emotions? As you vent, does it make you feel better? The answer should be no; I don't think that approach can make you feel better. In fact, it makes you feel worse.

Now do you understand the impact of judging your emotions? It keeps you on a roller coaster of emotions and increases emotional pain. Not sure of this? Okay, next time you have an argument with your friend or something happens with your parents, try venting to someone about it. Retell the story and use those judgments the way you normally would. However, this time, really notice yourself as you vent. Be aware of what happens to your emotions and your internal experience. Are they the same throughout the process of telling the story? Is there a decrease or an increase? Do you feel calm and relaxed, or do you feel tense? Does your voice remain calm as you tell the story, or do you notice the volume of your voice changing as you speak? After you've finished venting, do you feel better, worse, or the same?

Research has revealed that venting out will only make you relive the experience, which means those painful emotions will increase as you tell the story, and this can make you feel worse rather than better.

Below are some mindfulness exercises that can help you reduce your physical and emotional pain, make you feel relaxed and calm, increase positive emotions (self-control, memory, and concentration), and ultimately help you find balance.

Exercise: Mindful Listening

This exercise aims to enhance your hearing ability in a non-judgmental way and train your mind to not sway as a result of misconceptions and past experiences. You may not be aware of it, but what you feel right now may be influenced by your past experiences. For example, you dislike a particular song because it reminds you of a breakup that ended badly, so you tend to be sad any time you hear the song. The idea of this exercise is to experience the trigger from a neutral point. In this case, we'll use a song; listen to a song with the presence of your awareness and without any preconception.

Choose a song you've never listened to before. You can just go online or use the radio to choose a song that catches your ear.

- Put on your headphones and close your eyes.
- Before listening to the song, ensure you don't get drawn into judging the music by its title, genre, or artist. Ignore any of these labels and free yourself by getting lost in the song's rhythm and sound.
- Explore all aspects of the track without any reservations. You may not like the music at first but try to let go of the dislike and allow yourself to be fully aware as you enter into the track, dancing among the waves of the song.
- Listen to every dynamic of every instrument used in the song. In your mind, separate each sound and analyze them one after the other.
- Home in on the vocals, including the tone of the voice, sound, and range. Separate the voices if there is more than one.

The aim of this exercise is for you to listen with intention and become fully entwined in the composition of the song without any form of judgment. You don't need to think, just hear.

Exercise: Mindful Eating

Mindful eating involves paying attention to the food you are about to eat, noticing how it feels in your hands, focusing on its weight, texture, and color, and bringing about an awareness of its smell. This also involves chewing your food slowly, with full concentration. You should also notice the texture and taste against your tongue. This exercise will help you discover new experiences with foods.

Below is an assessment of your mindful eating skills. This assessment will help you identify the skills you need to improve and those you are already doing well with.

Tick (✓) the option that applies to you best.

I stop eating when I am full

At all times:
Most times:
Occasionally:
Sometimes:
Almost never:

I pick or graze on food

> *At all times:*
>
> *Most times:*
>
> *Occasionally:*
>
> *Sometimes:*
>
> *Almost never:*

I eat when I am hungry, not when I am emotional

> *At all times:*
>
> *Most times:*
>
> *Occasionally:*
>
> *Sometimes:*
>
> *Almost never:*

I am nonjudgmental of my body when I accidentally overeat

> *At all times:*
>
> *Most times:*
>
> *Occasionally:*
>
> *Sometimes:*
>
> *Almost never:*

I taste every bite of food properly before reaching for the next

> *At all times:*
>
> *Most times:*
>
> *Occasionally:*
>
> *Sometimes:*
>
> *Almost never:*

I think about the nourishment the food gives my body when I eat

> *At all times:*
>
> *Most times:*
>
> *Occasionally:*
>
> *Sometimes:*
>
> *Almost never:*

I don't do any other thing when I eat; I just eat

> *At all times:*
>
> *Most times:*
>
> *Occasionally:*
>
> *Sometimes:*
>
> *Almost never:*

I eat slowly and chew every bite

At all times:
Most times:
Occasionally:
Sometimes:
Almost never:

I don't have to eat everything on my plate; I can stop eating when I am full

At all times:
Most times:
Occasionally:
Sometimes:
Almost never:

I do realize when I zone out when eating and carefully guide my focus to the food

At all times:
Most times:
Occasionally:
Sometimes:
Almost never:

What are your mindful eating goals?

(Example: slowing down when eating, being more present, or stopping when full).

- _____
- _____
- _____

Exercise: Observe-a-Leaf Mindfulness

This very simple mindfulness exercise requires just your attention and a leaf. To do this:

- Pick a leaf and hold it in your hand.
- Focus on the leaf for five minutes, giving it your full attention.
- Notice the shape, color, patterns, and texture of the leaf.

This simple exercise will bring your awareness to the present and connect your thoughts with your present experience.

Exercise: Mindfulness Breathing

Many mindfulness breathing exercises can help you. So, I will be explaining some of those that are easy to practice.

Square Breathing:

- Breath in and hold your breath for four seconds.
- Breath out for four seconds.
- Repeat the process four times, and that's it!

Deep Breathing:

- Breath in through your nose.
- Breath out through your mouth.
- Quiet your mind and increase your focus by saying "in" when you breathe in and "out" when you breathe out.

Breathing Colors:

- Choose two colors (one for breathing in and one for breathing out).
- Picture a color for the breath-in and the other for the breath-out.
- Choose the colors you want and for the reasons you want them.
- Now, close your eyes and pair the colors with your breaths.

Belly Breathing:

- Lie down on the floor or bed, or just sit upright in a chair.
- Place your hands on your belly.

- Slowly breathe in and watch how your belly is expanding.

When you breathe this way, you promote deep breathing, which aids the transportation of oxygen into your system. You need more oxygen for relaxation and thinking clearly.

3-Step Mindfulness Worksheet

This worksheet is designed to help you practice mindfulness in three steps and bring your awareness to the present.

1. Step Away from Autopilot

In the first step, you will be bringing your awareness to what you are thinking, doing, and sensing at the moment. You will need to pause, stay in a comfortable position, be relaxed, and breathe.

What do you feel right now? What are the thoughts coming up in your mind?

Once you've identified them, give them your attention and notice them as natural experiences. Allow them to pass; slowly adjust to your current state and who you are.

2. Be Aware of Your Breath

Your goal at the moment is to be aware of your breath.

As you breathe in and out, how does your body move? Is your chest rising as you let air in and falling as you let the air out?

Once you know the pattern of your breath, anchor yourself to the present moment with what you've realized and take six breaths.

3. Expand Your Awareness Outwardly

In the last stage, you should allow your awareness to spread outwardly. It should start with your body and with your surroundings.

What are those physical sensations you are experiencing? Take note of any aches, feelings of lightness, or tightness, and let them go.

Now expand your awareness outwardly. Focus your attention on what's in front of you.

What shapes, colors, and textures can you notice?

Notice and be present in the awareness of those things.

Exercise: Mindful Immersion (Attention Workout)

This exercise aims to help you cultivate contentment with the moment and escape the constant hardship you get caught up in daily. It encourages you to engage in your regular routine and fully experience it, rather than anxiously wanting to get done with it to enable you to start something else.

The exercise encourages creativity so you can discover new experiences while doing a certain task. Whether you are cleaning your house or doing any other task, the aim is to pay attention to every little detail and notice every aspect of the task and your actions. For example, when sweeping the floor, you should feel and become the motion involved. You could sense your muscles as you scrub the dishes or have an efficient way of wiping a window clean.

Now, think of those routines you do daily. It can be taking a shower, washing, gardening, folding clothes, walking, brushing your teeth, and eating.

Write down any of the routines and where you want to do them.

It's time to write where your attention is focused. Is it self-focused attention (focused on your thoughts, feelings, emotions, and symptoms) or task-focused emotion (focused on the task)?

- Start doing the task without intentionally bringing your attention to it.
- Whenever you notice that your attention is wandering away from the task, carefully move your attention back to it without any form of judgment. Focus on:

Taste: What flavors do you notice? How many of them? Are they constant, or do they change during the task?

Sight: What are the things you can notice about the task? How does the task look? What catches your attention? Do you notice light, colors, and shadows?

Smell: What smell do you notice most? How many smells can you notice? Is the smell constant, or does it change during the task?

Touch: What task do you engage in? What does doing it feel like? What is the texture like? Is it rough or smooth? What part of your body are you using for the task?

_____

_____

_____

Hearing: What sounds can you notice? What sounds can you link to the task?

_____

_____

_____

_____

_____

_____

After completing this task, where did you notice your attention focused during the task?

_____

_____

_____

_____

_____

_____

What have you learned from the task, and what's your con-
clusion about the task?

_____

_____

_____

_____

_____

_____

You don't need to write down your answers to every
question above if you choose not to. I've provided them
to remind you that you need awareness of all your
sense organs during every task. You can use the senses

to shift your awareness back to the task when it wanders.

Finally, you can practice the act of mindfulness when in any difficult situation. In fact, you can practice it any time. Mindfulness doesn't advocate perfection; it's just about practicing how to improve your awareness of things. As you practice mindfulness, be compassionate with yourself. Life won't always be rosy. There are stressful times too, but you will feel better despite the difficulties when you use compassion and mindfulness.

CHAPTER 5:
MANAGING ANXIETY, ANGER, TRAUMA, AND PTSD WITH DBT

Even though DBT is popular for treating borderline personality disorder (BPD), it has a simple foundation. The concept is used for fostering change and acceptance. It allows people with other mental health conditions, such as anxiety, depression, anger, trauma, and PTSD, to accept the present, knowing that their future must be changed.

Managing Anxiety and Depression with DBT

One in every five Americans has a form of anxiety or an anxiety disorder. However, the good news is that research has revealed that DBT is very effective in helping anxious people manage their anxiety and live better lives.

With DBT, you can either work independently or with a therapist to find and resolve the contradictions between your present and your desired state of being. You will get a treatment plan that encourages positive behavioral changes.

The following are DBT techniques you can use to manage anxiety.

One-mindedness

This is a skill that encourages being in the moment. People often live in their present life thinking and worrying about their past or future. This can trigger anxiety as you get yourself stuck in thinking about what you've done wrong or what you think you will do wrong.

Being in the present moment will prepare you to better handle future problems and not worry about the past. When you worry constantly, it can be crippling— damaging your psyche to the extent that it becomes difficult to recognize effective actions or follow through with them.

When you engage fully in the present, you can easily deal with future issues that may arise. You also get to keep anxiety at bay because you will be fostering fewer worries about the past and so have a more mentally-grounded perspective to deal with future problems.

Exercise: Mindfulness of your current thoughts

Observe your thoughts:

- Notice as the waves come and go.
- Don't suppress, analyze, or judge your thoughts.
- Acknowledge the presence of your thoughts.
- Don't keep your thoughts around.
- Step away and observe your thoughts as they come in and escape your mind.

Have a curious mind:

- Ask yourself where your thoughts are coming from.
- Acknowledge that each thought that comes to your mind also goes out.
- Observe your thoughts without evaluating them.

Know that you aren't your thoughts:

- Don't act on your thoughts.
- Remember the times when you had different thoughts.
- Acknowledge that a catastrophic thought is from an emotional mind.
- Remember how you think when you don't feel pain and suffering.

Don't suppress your thoughts:

- Figure out the sensations your thoughts are trying to block off.
- Focus on the sensations and return to the thoughts after a moment.
- Step away by allowing your thoughts to come and go while observing your breath.
- Start playing with your thoughts by repeating them out loud as fast as you can.
- Love your thoughts.

Self-Soothing

This is the act of calming your emotional roller coaster by grounding yourself using your five senses. Most times, anxious people can easily get stuck in the emotional turmoil of their minds. You can escape your mind and enter the physical world again with the self-soothing technique. Instead of worrying and ruminating, DBT encourages you to gain relief through your senses.

Exercise: Self-soothing with the senses

In the worksheet below, write down pleasurable ways to soothe yourself. Write the fun things you would like to do when experiencing a difficult day.

Senses	Activities
Taste	Example: Chew gum or drink a cup of tea. • _____ • _____
Sight	Example: Watch my favorite movie or sit outside and bask in nature. • _____ • _____
Sound	Example: Listen to my favorite song or positive affirmations. • _____ • _____
Smell	Example: Light up a scented candle or diffuse essential oils • _____ • _____

Touch	Example: Take a warm bath or get a massage
	• _____
	• _____

Radical Acceptance

This technique requires you to accept the world exactly the way it is at the moment. I know that may sound easy, but it isn't. How easy is it to accept a painful breakup, the death of a loved one, or failing an exam?

The scope behind radical acceptance isn't to turn your back on the painful experiences but to accept that they happened; they are real and true. Therefore, your mental effort should be focused on making peace with an experience or changing it.

Exercise: Improving the moment

When faced with anxiety, you should improve the moment by:

- **Imagining** yourself dealing with the problem successfully
- Finding **meaning** in the difficult situation
- **Praying** to a higher power asking for strength to tolerate the pain a little longer

- **Relaxing**
- Focusing on **one thing** at a time
- **Vacationing** in your mind
- **Encouraging** yourself

So how can you apply this?

Imagining	Visualize a secret room within yourself or a relaxing scene. Daydream about your favorite place or memory.
Meaning	Recall the important things in your life. What can you learn from the tough times you've experienced? Have you survived a similar situation before?
Praying	Meditate, pray, or ponder about it. Use your spirituality.
Relaxing	Use calming techniques such as deep breathing. Don't prevent the event; allow it to unfold.
Being in the moment	Be aware of what you are doing in the moment and focus on one thing at a time.
Vacationing	Take a break.

Encouraging	Use positive affirmations or make helpful statements about yourself and others.

Exercise: Pros and cons list

This exercise entails making a list of the pros and cons of a situation to help you decide if you should act on the anxiety-based urge or go with a healthier decision.

	Pros	Cons
Coping	<ul><li>No argument</li><li>No fight</li><li>Gaining others' trust</li><li>Having more privileges</li><li>Increased self-esteem</li><li>Maintain relationship</li></ul>	<ul><li>You don't get to argue or fight</li><li>You fail to make your point</li><li>There's no instant gratification</li><li>Others won't fear you</li></ul>
Not Coping	<ul><li>You will be left alone</li><li>Hurting someone</li><li>Instant gratification</li><li>Feeling powerful</li></ul>	<ul><li>Low self-worth</li><li>Lost self-esteem</li><li>Lost respect</li><li>Lost motivation for getting treated</li><li>Rebellion against using skills</li></ul>

Now, ask yourself which of the pros and cons listed above are short-term (one day) and which are long-term (more than one day). If you've identified them, ask your wise mind if you would rather experience a good day or a good life. Then make a mindful choice of action.

Making sensible decisions when you're anxious can be difficult. Using the pros and cons list can help individuals decide if they should act on an anxiety-based urge or develop a healthier decision.

Exercise: TIPP

TIPP is an acronym that stands for temperature, intense exercise, paced breathing, and paired muscle relaxation.

You can practice TIPP when you experience anxiety by:

- Cooling your body **temperature** (this calms you emotionally too)
- Practicing an **intense exercise** to match your intense emotions
- **Pacing** your breathing
- Engaging in **paired muscle relaxation**

The exercises I've shared can help you prepare for intense emotions and cope with distressing feelings in a better way.

Managing Anger with DBT

If you experience anger that turns into rage, say things in the heat of the moment and eventually regret it, or are looking for coping strategies to help you cope with your anger, then this section is for you.

Anger can be damaging to the extent that it affects what you do or say before you can even recognize the emotion. When you express anger all the time, you may get so used to the emotion that you don't notice when it's there. The first step to take when managing anger is identifying those warning signs that tell you how you feel.

When you are angry, how do you react? Some warning signs may show themselves when you feel a little irritated, while others show up when you are very angry.

Tick (✓) the warning signs that apply to you in the following table.

Warning signs

Face turns red

Mind goes blank

Insult the person

Scream or yell

Throw things

Argue

Hand and body shake

Punch walls

Start sweating

Cry

Become aggressive

Headaches

Pace around

Feel hot inside

The next exercise offers steps you can take to overcome the anger.

Know your anger sign	Use the list of warning signs above to know your anger sign.
Take a time-out	Leave the situation that's making you angry, even if temporarily. Take a few minutes to calm down.

Engage in deep breathing	Practice deep breathing by counting your breaths. Inhale and count four seconds; exhale and count four seconds.
Exercise	Exercise triggers chemicals to be released in your brain to create a sense of happiness and relaxation.
Express your anger	Express your frustration after calming down. Be assertive and not aggressive.
Know the consequences of your anger	What can be the result of your anger-fueled actions? Will throwing things convince the person that you are right? Will you be happy with your actions?
Visualize a better outcome	Imagine having a relaxed experience. What can you see, hear, smell, taste, and touch? Spend a few minutes imagining being in your ideal environment.

Managing Trauma and PTSD with DBT

Whether you are suffering from panic attacks, unrelenting worries, or a phobia due to trauma and PTSD, you don't need to continue living this way. With DBT, you don't need to burden your mind with worries or live in fear. DBT encourages people living with trauma to face their fears rather than avoid them. Exposing yourself to fearful thoughts and situations will eventually reduce the pain that comes with them.

But how can you do this, especially when it's very uncomfortable? The following exercises will help you manage your feelings and live a better life.

Exercise: Assess your limitations

This exercise aims to assess your limitation of trauma-provoking thoughts and situations. The response you give will encourage you to break free from the shackles of your past.

What thoughts or situations have prevented you from pursuing your goals and living your best life?

How would you act differently if you overcame this experience and focused on what's important?

What are your thoughts and feelings when faced with the experience?

What steps can you take to overcome the trauma?

List five things you can do to face trauma-based thoughts.

After accomplishing the steps listed, how can you use them to manage trauma in the future?

Exercise: Work through the trauma and live your best life

This exercise entails doing certain activities to help you work through your trauma, stop being a hostage of your thoughts, and start living your best life.

Sit with your fear: When the thoughts come, don't avoid them. Just sit with them for three minutes. Remind yourself that being scared is natural, and you will eventually be in charge of your thoughts. After three minutes, start doing an activity you enjoy, such as singing, dancing, or painting.

Encourage yourself: When a difficult and painful thought comes, tell yourself that you won't allow fear to limit you or prevent you from achieving your goals. Remind yourself of how strong you are and that you shouldn't be stopped and attacked by your thoughts.

Start exercising: Start engaging in exercise to help you refocus your mind toward more important things. Go for a walk, do yoga, or start dancing. This will also boost the confidence you need to face any situation.

Write a gratitude list: Your gratitude list should contain the things that make you grateful. When you feel down and in a bad place, look at the list and recall the things you have that you're thankful for. This will make you feel better.

Use humor to deflate your worries: Use humor to reduce your fears and worries when discomforting thoughts appear. For example, when thinking of the heartbreak you experienced and how you were jilted, you can say to yourself, *"What's the worst-case scenario? He probably wasn't the one for me, and I know I will love again."* Or, when you lose a loved one, you can say, *"Death is a natural phenomenon that will happen to us all. Maybe not now, but eventually."*

CHAPTER 6:
THE ROAD TO POSITIVE EMOTIONS
(IMPROVING YOUR MOOD)

From the beginning of this book, we've been discussing skills that can help you manage painful and discomforting emotions and prevent you from experiencing emotional pain. I believe you've been practicing these skills and have started seeing results, no matter how small. Meanwhile, there is an important aspect we need to discuss, and that is your mood. Unfortunately, despite the skills you've learned and practiced, your mood will likely not improve unless you focus on seeking to improve it.

You probably think this is another process that requires hard work, and you aren't sure if you are up for that. But doesn't feeling better require hard work? If you regularly feel anxious, depressed, nervous, angry, irritated, annoyed, and traumatized, then you need to put in the work to improve your mood and slow down the emotional rollercoaster you've been riding. This is what this final chapter will focus on—smoothing out the rollercoaster ride by improving your mood.

First, we'll start with having a goal and working toward it before other steps can follow.

Work Toward a Goal

If you want to improve your mood and your life in general, goal setting is important. You are heading toward failure if you live a life without goals. Therefore, it is important to set goals that will encourage accountability.

Goal-setting can help you face emotional and behavioral challenges, improve your savings habits, score better grades in school, and build better relationships. It is your roadmap to success when trying to overcome challenges and live a better life.

To help you set effective goals, we'll be discussing the SMART rule, which stands for making your goals Specific, Measurable, Achievable, Realistic, and Time-bound.

Set SMART Goals

There are different approaches to executing your plans, and an effective one is the SMART way. Setting SMART goals will give you a better idea of your objectives and encourage you to achieve them.

Exercise: Making your goals SMART

Write your response in the box below.

SPECIFIC

What would you like to achieve? Ensure your goal is specific and broken down into smaller steps.

MEASURABLE

Write how you can make your goals measurable. How would you know when your aims have been achieved? What difference do you expect? What will you be doing seldom and doing regularly?

ACHIEVABLE

What are the achievable goals you can set to avoid failure? You can set smaller goals and celebrate when you achieve a milestone.

REALISTIC

What resources do you have at your disposal? Are they enough to achieve your goals? Do you need extra resources? If you do, do you have access to them or not? What challenges do you experience when accessing them? What are the steps you need to take to remove these challenges?

TIME-BOUND

What is the reasonable timeline you can set for achieving your goals? The timeline can be a day, a week, a month, a year, or more. Break down the goals and note a timeline for each of the steps.

What changes can you effect to improve your mood and your life generally? Write them down below.

1. Changes with family:

_____

2. Changes at school:

_____

3. Changes with friends:

_____

4. Changes in extra-curriculum activities (music, sports, and work):

_____

What would you like to focus on first?

_____

_____

_____

What are your possible obstacles?

What can you do to overcome these obstacles?

When do you want to make these changes?

If you aren't sure that the SMART rule for goal setting will be helpful, or if you can't seem to set meaningful goals by using it, you can switch your plan and use another technique for goal setting. Use a technique that has a solid plan and will give results.

If you want to see results with SMART goal setting, you will need to be patient with the process. Though it may take time, especially with long-term goals. I encourage you to hang in there and be patient with the process.

In your planning, don't try to comply with "all or nothing" rules because you have a variety of goals, and you can't achieve all of them at once. Not achieving them at the same time doesn't mean you are a failure. Celebrate the little ones you've achieved and prepare for the bigger ones. When you fail to achieve a goal, take your time to have a better plan in place to prevent failure the next time you attempt it.

Building Mastery

While goal setting is important, you need to engage in pleasurable activities to strike a balance and make you feel fulfilled. The DBT skill of building mastery encourages you to engage in activities that will make you feel productive and proud of yourself for achieving something. The list for building mastery mustn't be the same as that of anyone else; it's different for everyone. While it may be auditioning for the school play for one person, it could be making it to school on time for another. What really matters is that the activity should give you a pleasant and positive feeling about yourself.

Think about what you are doing in your life that gives you a positive and pleasurable feeling. What else can you do to make sure you have this sense of fulfillment regularly?

Engaging in Pleasurable Activities

It's advisable to engage in different activities to boost your mood and achieve mental wellness. According to studies, exercises can help produce endorphins in your body. Endorphins are feel-good hormones that boost your mood and make you happy and energized. Examples of such exercises include breathing practices, yoga, meditation, visualization, and other fun activities. Engaging in any exercise regularly is beneficial to your health and state of mind.

The following are activities you can engage in:

Focused Hobbies

This involves taking some time off to read articles, paint, walk, watch a movie, learn a musical instrument, or go shopping. Get yourself a hobby that will take your thoughts off your usual routine. The idea is to refresh and re-energize your mind. If you need to change your environment to get it done, don't hesitate to do that.

Visualization

Imagine yourself in a calm and relaxed place. This can be lying on a beach, sitting on top of a mountain, or lounging under a tree. While you are in this calm state, what can you see? What can you taste? What can you feel? What can you smell? What can you hear? What are your thoughts? Your discovery should make you feel relaxed and able to enjoy the moment.

Deep Breathing

We've discussed practicing deep breathing in Chapters 4 and 5, so you should be familiar with it already. Deep breathing entails focusing your attention on your breath for a few minutes. Inhale through your nose and count to four, hold your breath for four seconds, exhale through your mouth, and count for another four seconds.

Improve Your Relationships

As you survive the emotional roller coaster and learn skills that will help you manage your emotions more beneficially, it's pertinent to improve your relationship with your friends, family, teacher, coaches, and love interests. This can positively affect your mood and influence how well you manage your emotions.

We are social creatures that need people around us. When you have healthy and satisfying relationships, you can be more emotionally resilient. The people around you greatly influence your feelings, so it's important to continually improve the bond you have with them.

A major component of DBT is interpersonal effectiveness, or improving your relationship with others. Therefore, the following techniques aim to help you accomplish that.

GIVE Skills

The GIVE skills entail:

- Be **gentle.** Be nice and respectful and avoid any form of physical and verbal attacks. Don't engage in gestures that are insulting and threatening. For example, don't roll your eyes, clench your fists, smirk, or hiss.
- Be **interested**. Even when you aren't absorbed in what the other person is saying, act interested by maintaining eye contact and giving listening ears. Don't interrupt or talk over them.
- **Validate** them. When you validate, you show that you understand their point of view and why they do what they do.
- Use an **easy manner.** Remember to use easy manners such as humor and smiling.

FAST Skills

These skills will help you preserve your self-respect when interacting with others. To do this:

- Be **fair** to yourself and others. Appreciate your worth and needs.

- Don't over-**apologize**. This doesn't mean you shouldn't apologize when you are at fault. It means you shouldn't apologize for having a different opinion or asking for what you need.

- **Stick** to your values. Communicate what you believe in clearly, and don't be afraid to stand up for your opinion when it comes to your values.

- Be **truthful** and don't lie. When you lie to get what you want, you will compromise your relationship with others and lose self-respect.

DEAR MAN

This is an interpersonal skill that you can use to ask for what you want, respectfully and effectively, thereby building and maintaining wholesome relationships with others, regardless of whether or not you get what you asked for.

To do this:

- **Describe** the situation simply. If you want to go shopping with your friend, you can describe the situation in a straightforward way by saying, "My friends are going to the mall to shop for new clothes this weekend."

- **Express** what you would like to do. For example, "I would like to go shopping with them."

- **Assert** respectfully and not aggressively why it is important to you. For example, "I haven't spent time with my friends since track season started, so it would mean a lot if I could go with them this weekend."

- **Reinforce** when you get what you asked for. For example, "I promise to do all my homework before I leave for shopping."

- **Mindfully** stay in the moment. Don't worry about your past or future; just be in the moment. For example, don't worry about what your friends will say if you cancel going out.

- **Appear** confident. Don't be afraid to ask your friends to give you more time to focus on your homework instead, if that's what you need. Approach the situation confidently.

- **Negotiate** if it looks like you won't get your desired result. Many teenagers aren't used to asking for something; they would rather make demands and ask in uncertain ways that seem confusing. Or they would rather not ask at all and just do what they want. So, it's important to be flexible and find a happy middle ground for both yourself and the other person.

Interpersonal effectiveness skills aren't just for helping those struggling with BPD; it is helpful for anyone who wants to strengthen the relationships they have with the people around them.

FINAL WORDS

Well done! You've finally reached the end of this book, and I must commend you for staying with me all the way. It's been an exciting experience, walking through this journey with you, and I believe you've learned the invaluable skills of DBT. These skills will help you make positive changes in your life and achieve mental wellness.

I believe that you now know:

- What DBT entails and how you can utilize its skills
- How to identify the times when you have unhealthy thoughts and the exercises you can use to focus on the moment instead of acting on those thoughts
- Important strategies you can use to manage anxiety, anger, trauma, and PTSD

- How to reevaluate your life and set goals for the next stage of your life
- How to improve your mood by engaging in pleasurable activities
- How to build better relationships

You might encounter obstacles along the way as you strive to live a healthier and better life. However, I trust you won't give up and let the hard work you've invested in this journey go to waste. Keep moving forward, and you will get your reward shortly.

I've shared effective skills, techniques, and exercises to improve your mental health. As with any form of therapy, DBT requires work on your part. So I encourage you not to give up; keep practicing what you've learned in this book, and in no time, you will get your desired results.

Thank you,
The Mentor Bucket

DOWNLOADABLE WORKSHEETS

Go to the below URLs to download all worksheets (in pdf format) given in the book - 1.

www.thementorbucket.com/dbt-ws1.pdf

BOOK - 2

DBT SKILLS WORKBOOK
FOR PARENTS OF TEENS

A Proven Strategy for Understanding and
Parenting Adolescents Who Suffer from
Intense Emotions, Anger, and Anxiety

The Mentor Bucket

INTRODUCTION

D o you feel tired and exhausted and sometimes regret being a parent? Perhaps your child had once driven you to the point of no return with your emotions, and you had to lash out.

No doubt, parenting can be quite overwhelming, especially when you have a teenager who drives you over the roof by throwing tantrums when you are out together, foot-stomping when a request is denied, having constant meltdowns, being too embarrassed to speak up, and constantly feeling anxious about little things.

The adolescent ages are fraught with many intense emotions that can pose problems for teens who don't know how to manage them. Research has revealed that the ability of a child to cope with the uncertainties of life plays a significant role in their social and academic success, making it important for parents to improve their parenting skills by learning how to tame these emotions and ensure their kids don't lose control of them.

Knowing how to regulate intense emotions involves tolerating difficult feelings such as disappointment and knowing how to react in different social situations. Skills for managing emotions will help a teen be in control of these emotions and act better when they are faced with difficult situations.

I am guessing also that no one told you parenting would be this challenging. Well, many of us weren't told this either, so we just had to learn to be better parents on the job.

As parents, you have an important role in developing and modeling coping skills for your teens, even though many adults are not aware of the basics of emotional intelligence. Unfortunately, many parents have inherited traits of unhealthy coping strategies – including avoidance, yelling, or suppressing emotions – and this puts their children at risk of inheriting the same garbage.

Even skilled parents with high emotional intelligence still find it difficult to parent a teen who exhibits intense emotions. Emotions can be extreme and often unpredictable. They can even turn on a dime.

While managing intense emotions can be difficult, there is hope!

If your child's traits are beginning to escalate into dangerous and aggressive behaviors – such as binging, cutting, throwing things, refusing, threatening, and responding negatively to limits and expectations – you are probably confused and scared already. Don't be scared or feel alone in this situation—many other parents have reported having difficulty managing teenagers with intense emotions, anger, and anxiety.

I was once like you, filled with many questions about how to be in control of one's emotions. I was scared of losing myself until I was introduced to Dialectal Behavioral Therapy (DBT) skills and strategies.

Many times, I have wondered why my child has such intense emotions. It's easy for them to scream because they can't have their way, cry when everyone else is having a good time, look at me with anger on their face when I try correcting them, and see homework as a nightmare. Like you, I finally got to a point where I was scared to tell my child NO.

While the behaviors I have described may differ slightly from what your child is experiencing, these are all signs showing that your child suffers from emotional dysregulation. Children with emotional dysregulation tend to react intensely and quickly to circumstances and situations that others don't react to. They will also face a hard time returning to their former, initial state. We can describe children like these as *going from 0 to 100 in split seconds.*

If you've been disturbed by and worried about your child's behaviors and responses to emotions they can't seem to manage in positive ways, parenting with DBT can actually help! It saved me from the nightmare I was in by changing my life and that of my child — for good!

DBT is a skilled therapy structured to help people with intense emotions live better lives. These skills help individuals achieve their goals by reducing behaviors that prevent them from achieving those goals in the first place. With DBT, you can understand and effectively respond to your child's behaviors and emotions.

Parents are taught the idea of emotions, where they come from, and how they function. This helps increase awareness and boost interaction between parents and their children. As parents, you need to learn what makes your teen vulnerable to the intense emotions, triggers, and beliefs that influence their emotional responses. Observe how intense and negative emotions affect your child and how these pose problems. Then you can intervene early and respond with greater acceptance and a good understanding. This allows you to be more effective in helping your child have more control over their emotions and feel better.

DBT teaches you four important skills modules: emotion regulation, mindfulness, interpersonal effectiveness, and distress tolerance. In the modules, you will learn how to help your teens focus their attention, regulate their painful emotions, and deal with distress. You will also find effective strategies for coping with interpersonal conflict.

You can improve your child's behaviors by shaping them with constructive activities, using positive reinforcements and contracts to maintain expectations and limits, and using punishment minimally.

Combining the right information, specific skills, and a nonjudgmental approach will definitely give results. The goal is to live an enjoyable and meaningful life with your family. Even though your family life might differ from your initial vision, DBT provides an increased calm in your life and encourages a well-knit relationship with your child.

Parenting isn't black and white; there are many factors involved in making decisions, so it's not fitting to merely choose one extreme over another. DBT encourages parents to parent from a more balanced perspective, and DBT aims to teach this as well. The word "dialectical" means finding a balance between acceptance and change. This encourages an environment of collaboration and flexibility by teaching your teenagers that while some things are changeable, depending on the circumstances, other things are absolutes.

Rather than downplay the problematic behaviors, or overly focus on normal adolescent development, there is a balance between knowing when a behavior crosses a line and when the behavior is just a typical part of adolescent development. This way, you will know whether to seek professional help or not.

Parents often struggle with maintaining balance in their relationship with their teens as a result of encouraging too much dependence, allowing too much independence, fostering overly close relationships, and not giving enough guidance to their child.

If you are at one end of the spectrum, it's time to find a balance by providing your teen with the right guidance and support while teaching them to take appropriate responsibility. As you step back to increase your child's independence, try to encourage structure at the same time.

Initially, avoiding the black and white, rigid parenting style may be difficult. However, you can do it. With practice, patience, and an altered mindset, you are on track! You will realize that taking a dialectical approach will greatly improve your relationship with your teen.

This book will discuss how you can use some carefully selected DBT strategies and skills to be in more control and live a peaceful life with your teen. If you can help them manage their behaviors and emotions more efficiently, your child will experience a trickle-down effect.

First, I will explain what DBT entails by discussing the modules, the formation of your child's emotions, and the connection between thought, behavior, and feelings.

Also, we'll discuss if emotional dysregulation is just a phase or a real problem in your young one's life and what to do in either case. In this important journey, you must understand your child's emotions, and we'll be discussing their causes, some warning signs, and when to seek help for your child. I'll also present you with effective strategies to help you manage your child's emotions.

Finally, you'll kickstart your new role of being an effective parent. You will learn what it means to be an effective parent, why it is a good way of parenting, how to respond to your child's behaviors and feelings, and various parenting strategies for your child with intense emotions.

My first encounter with DBT was during my years working as a clinician and helping both teenagers and parents battle severe and persistent mental illnesses. Many of the clients I had were battling anxiety, depression, anger, trauma, Post Traumatic Stress Disorder

(PTSD), and suicide. With my DBT training, I was able to help people and cater to their needs.

I know there are many people out there battling the same issues. I am writing this book to reach a wider audience, especially people experiencing emotional challenges and who want to set themselves free from the roller coaster of emotions. I designed this workbook to be simple, with complicated terms explained in bits. Inside, you will find exercises to engage in. Ensure you attend to these, as they are a significant part of this process.

So, are you ready to start this exciting journey with me? Flip to the next page, where we'll be discussing DBT and what it entails.

CHAPTER 1:
UNDERSTANDING DBT

Since the start of the 20th century, psychotherapy has witnessed three evolutions: the development of behavioral therapy, which took place in the 1950s, the development of Aaron Beck's cognitive therapy in the 1970s, and the merging of both therapies to present a more contemporary therapy called the cognitive behavioral therapy (CBT). Over the last two decades, there has been an emergence of the "third wave" of cognitive and behavior therapy, which incorporates acceptance and mindfulness techniques.

Dialectical behavior therapy (DBT) is one of the third-wave therapies that have proven to be very effective in treating individuals with Borderline Personality Disorder (BPD) and those with difficulty regulating their emotions. DBT balances cognitive behavioral therapy and humanism using dialectics. Dr. Marsha Linehan developed this therapy in the 1970s after her personal experience with mental illness. DBT was the first psychotherapy to formally incorporate mindfulness into its practice.

What is DBT?

DBT, also known as dialectical behavioral therapy, is a talking therapy treatment performed through a group therapy session and one-on-one talks with individual therapists and a phone coach/therapist. It is based on cognitive behavior therapy but has been adapted to treat people suffering from intense emotions. It also helps struggling individuals identify and change their negative thinking patterns into positive ones.

DBT aims to help individuals:

- Understand and accept their difficult feelings
- Learn skills to help them manage these emotions
- Develop the ability to make positive changes in their lives

The term "Dialectical" in DBT means trying to understand how two opposing things could both be true. For example, the idea of accepting yourself and also changing your behavior may seem contradictory. However, DBT teaches us that both goals can be achieved together.

DBT has about six points that work together. As a patient using DBT, you are advised not to think too far into the future because that can trigger episodes such as destructive behaviors, depressive states, suicidal behaviors, and eating disorders.

Instead, individuals are taught healthy and positive ways of dealing with stress and intense emotions, regulating emotions, and improving relationships with loved ones. DBT aims to identify, change, and support individuals so they can cope with unhealthy and negative behaviors and emotions, especially in social situations.

Brief History of DBT

DBT was first founded in the 70s by Marsha Linehan, a suicide researcher at the time. Before then, she didn't know a lot about borderline personality disorder (BPD), but she became familiar with it later on. The researcher found the effectiveness of DBT in treating borderline personality disorder. Decades later, BPD practices seem to have become open to argument since DBT is now being used to treat many other mental health issues.

Linehan engaged her patients with real-world examples instead of having one-way conversations with them to get the desired responses. She succeeded in teaching her patients to react differently when in various situations. The process Linehan used removes the challenges that had been confusing therapists who were treating suicidal patients. Studies have revealed DBT as effective in treating self-injurious behavior and suicidal attempts. DBT is also used in treating drug and alcohol addiction. This therapy has shown positive results in patients within these groups. It is now a widely recognized and accepted form of therapy in different parts of the world.

DBT vs. CBT

Perhaps you've heard about CBT before, and at one point you've confused it to mean the same thing as DBT. Well, DBT is a form of CBT that differs in terms of skills.

With DBT, there is the addition of acceptance, mindfulness techniques, and no form of judgment. DBT eliminates the judgmental properties of CBT to ensure that the way an individual thinks isn't seen as wrong, distorted, or erroneous. The goal is to help individuals change how they think.

DBT acknowledges that a problem exists with how an individual thinks while encouraging them to accept this truth without judgment. This helps them seek ways to change their thinking to make it more healthy and balanced.

The model of DBT also shows that it's quite different from CBT. While DBT is a principle-driven therapy,

CBT is more of a protocol-based therapy. There are principles guiding DBT that allow flexibility for the therapist, whereas CBT follows stricter procedures. For example, when an individual has a panic attack, only certain rules are followed for the treatment, including abdominal breathing and psychoeducation. This isn't the case for DBT because it allows added flexibility.

Another difference between the two therapies is how the treatments are delivered. DBT has four modes of therapy: skills group, individual therapy, therapy team, and telephone consultation. CBT is provided in an individual format or a group session, and the two rarely occur simultaneously.

While both CBT and DBT incorporate self-monitoring, it is taken to a different level in DBT by using behavior tracking sheets. DBT also differs in the way the sessions are structured to address behavior and in how the stages of the treatment are determined by the threat and severity of the target behaviors.

The DBT Model

DBT consists of four main modules. However, my professional experience has shown me that DBT can be provided to clients effectively without including all the modules. Therefore, research on DBT for BPD acknowledges the complete model, including individual therapy, skills training groups, telephone consultation, and the consultation team.

Individual Therapy

Here, clients attend individual sessions with a therapist weekly. This individual therapy aims to help individuals utilize the skills they've learned in the group to reduce behaviors such as self-harm, suicide, and use of a substance. The individual session has a clear format and session.

Skills Training Group

This psychoeducational, structured group format aims to develop and improve an individual's capabilities. The skills training group is divided into four modules. They include interpersonal effectiveness skills, emotional regulation skills, distress tolerance skills, and core mindfulness skills.

Interpersonal effectiveness skills: These skills aim to help clients reduce the interpersonal chaos that is often present in their lives and is primarily about how to be more assertive. Clients are taught to think about what they most want to get out of interaction (for example, if they have a specific objective, if they wish to keep or even improve the relationship, or if they wish to keep or improve their self-respect), and then they are taught skills that will make it more likely for them to reach this goal.

Core mindfulness skills: In 1993, Linehan broke down the concept of mindfulness into smaller parts to ensure individuals could understand it and can easily incorporate it into their lives. Mindfulness was formerly used to treat BPD by reducing the confused perception of one's self. However, mindfulness has proven to be helpful in many more ways now. When individuals have increased awareness, they are aware of their emotions, thoughts, and urges.

Individuals can learn the skills of attempting to manage emotions efficiently and tolerating the emotions they can't do anything about. They will understand that they don't need to act on internal experience, but that a simple acknowledgment of the experiences will ensure they dissipate gradually.

Emotional regulation skills: The goal of emotional regulation skills is to reduce mood liability. Individuals are made to understand the workings of their emotions and other details such as why they need their emotions and why they shouldn't get rid of them even when they are very discomforting and painful. Individuals will also learn the connection between feelings, thoughts, and behaviors and understand that changing one of these will affect the others. In this module, self-validation and other skills to help individuals manage their emotions more effectively are emphasized.

Distress tolerance skills: The distress tolerance skills are also called the crisis survival skills. This module aims to help individuals survive crises without engaging in unhealthy behaviors such as self-harm, suicide attempts, and substance abuse. The skills will help individuals soothe and distract themselves from the issue instead of dwelling on it, since brooding on it will make them act on their urges and bring about painful emotions.

While these skills can be taught in individual therapy, they are addressed in a group format for several reasons. First, individuals with difficulty regulating their emotions often move from one crisis to another, making it extremely difficult to teach skills in an individual session when they need help with their current crisis. Validation is also an important aspect; individuals benefit from being in the same group as others with similar problems.

Learning can be more effective with group therapy since individuals learn from the experiences of other group members. In addition, since interpersonal issues surface in the group, it can be a great opportunity to practice the learned skills and allow individuals to receive coaching on how to use the skills to act more appropriately.

Telephone Consultation

This medium is used to coach individuals on using skills they've been taught. Telephone consultation is a brief interaction that aims at helping clients identify the skills that are more helpful in certain situations and how to overcome obstacles while using the skills effectively.

Consultation Team

Linehan has made it clear that DBT is incomplete without a team. The composition of a consultation team varies depending on the environment. Generally, the team consists of the therapists in a DBT clinic including psychologists, social workers, psychiatrists, and others working in the training group.

This is a straightforward process for therapists working in a clinical setting. However, it can be complicated for those working in private practice. The reason is simple! The team is needed to ensure therapists are on track with their practice. Therefore, therapists in private practice may need to form a team that consists of other private DBT therapists around them while ensuring that confidentiality is strictly adhered to.

As a practitioner in private practice, I am fortunate to have psychiatrists working in a DBT clinic to support me with consultations. The team size doesn't matter;

what's important is that the therapist receives objective feedback about their practice.

The DBT consultation team is used in two ways: providing support to therapists by pushing them to develop their skills in using the DBT model and coordinating case discussion. The team must ensure that the therapist adheres to DBT strategies and techniques in case discussion. They are also in charge of addressing feelings of burnout.

The team also uses DBT techniques such as being non-judgmental and taking a dialectal stance to prevent other team members from getting roped into power struggles that can disrupt the therapeutic process.

Exercise: Reason for Change

Before moving to the next section, now is a good time to think about your reason for reading this book. First, you need to identify those changes you want to make. So, in this exercise, you will write down three ways your child reacts to certain emotions — reactions you would want to change. This way, you become committed to replacing those behaviors with better ways of coping.

Write down three damaging things your child does when angry, anxious, or overwhelmed.

• ---

- --

- --

So, how could a better understanding of the things you have mentioned help you? Will it contribute to a better parenting experience?

- --

- --

- --

DBT skills and strategies can help you reduce the intensity of emotional waves and balance your emotions when they overwhelm you. We'll discuss that later.

Emotional Intensity and Your Child's Feelings

Does your teen throw tantrums and show displeasure by complaining or pouting? Do their demands become so relentless that you feel you have no other choice but to give in? Do you always wonder why your child is mostly emotional and tends to react intensely to situations that should've been ignored? Does it take very long for them to get over things?

Like adults, teens have emotions too. Their emotions are very real and not easily ignored. How you feel affects what you do, how you do it, and your perception of yourself. Knowing this makes understanding your child's intense behavioral responses important. Unfortunately, these are emotions they find hard to manage.

The following section will explain the driving force behind your child's behaviors and your reactions to those behaviors. Knowing this will position you in a good place to use the skills and strategies we'll be discussing in this book.

Primary and Secondary Emotions

Everyone (babies, teens, and adults) has primary and secondary emotions. While the primary emotions are based on biology and are almost automatic, the secondary emotions are created by reactions to primary emotions.

You don't have much control over your primary emotions, but you have a bit of control over the creation and perpetuation of secondary emotions. Your secondary emotions last longer than the primary ones, leading to more maladaptive behavioral responses.

Let's quickly look at how primary emotions happen and secondary emotions are created.

Primary Emotions Happen

Primary emotions include anger, fear, sadness, joy, disgust, and surprise. These emotions are usually hardwired in you. They are your first reaction and the emotions you feel when a situation affects you. You experience them physiologically as they come and go like waves on the shore.

Exercise: Primary Emotions

This exercise aims to help you understand primary emotions by looking at a situation that will likely make you experience primary emotions.

Imagine being called to your child's school by the principal. You don't have significant details, but it seems like your child got into a fight. While driving to school, you think about the situation.

What are those feelings you'd have while driving?

Secondary Emotions Are Created

Let's look at the example of being called by the principal of your child's school. You've listed the primary emotions you felt after hearing the news in the preceding exercise. The primary emotions may be fear, alarm, and anger, especially if this is not the first time hearing that your child got into a fight.

On arriving at the principal's office, you are informed that your child got hit by a classmate, and he wasn't the instigator. This makes you start thinking about the initial anger you felt and how you've erroneously jumped to conclusions. Your current thought will create a secondary emotion in you, which will likely be guilt.

Your secondary emotions are your reactions to your primary emotions. They are also the result of the assumptions and beliefs you learned throughout your life. For example, if during your younger years your parents showed disappointment when you felt a fit of unjustified anger, you may experience guilt whenever you feel anger. You can have many secondary emotions in response to one primary emotion; however, it might be so much and so overwhelming that you won't remember the primary emotions that triggered them.

Your Thoughts, Feelings, and Behaviors

No emotion occurs in isolation. Your emotions are a result of cognitive processes and physiological reactions. It's either something internal, which can be your thought, or something external, which can be an event that makes you experience an emotion. The emotions may pop up so quickly that you aren't even aware of the trigger/cause.

Thoughts lead to feelings, which lead to behaviors

Your feelings are directly related to your thoughts, which lead to your behavioral responses. Your thoughts are your internal beliefs, phrases, images, and attitudes. Some of your thoughts may happen so automatically that you aren't aware of their existence. On the other hand, feelings are the physiological reactions you experience that shape your present experience. The result of thoughts and feelings is behavior. Behavior is how you respond and act due to how you feel.

You definitely can't scan your child's head to know exactly what they think. You can see only their behaviors resulting from their feelings and thoughts. Since you aren't 100% certain of the feelings and thoughts behind the behavior, you will likely make some assumptions. Depending on different factors, your assumptions may either be accurate or not. Your child's reality and your assumptions may be totally different. As a result, your child may find it difficult to express themselves and share exactly how they are feeling or why they are feeling it. We'll be discussing this later in this book, where you'll learn ways to help your child be more vocal in telling you how they feel.

To understand the connection between thoughts, feelings, and behaviors, let's quickly look at an example below, which describes how different thoughts about the same event can lead to different behaviors and feelings.

When your child isn't doing what you want them to do (event), you start thinking:

"Why do my words always fall on deaf ears? Why must we always go through this anytime he needs to do something?" You may get angry (your feeling) and lash out (your behavior).

Or

"Okay, I will let this slide since he is having a bad day."

In this case, you may feel relieved (your feeling) and get over it (your behavior).

In the example above, what you told yourself about the event (your thoughts) has affected your feelings and behavior.

By being aware of your thoughts, you will have the skills needed to change your behavioral and emotional responses to situations.

On the other hand, regardless of being aware or not, your child also responds to *their* thoughts. The example below will explain how different thoughts can lead to a behavioral and emotional response in a teen.

Your child sees a boy he recognizes (event). Then, he thinks, *"Is the boy ignoring me?"* (thought). Then, he gets sad (emotion) and slowly withdraws from that situation (event).

Or

Perhaps, your child says out loud, *"The boy there is my friend!"* (thought). He is happy (emotion) and approaches the boy to say hello (behavior).

As you can see, what you think about a situation affects how you feel and behave in that instance.

Your child is not their behavior

Behaviors aren't constant; they can be changed. Your child's behavioral responses are usually learned and are not inborn or ingrained in their personalities. Learning about and understanding your child depends on how you separate your child from their behaviors. Your child is not their behavior. Their behaviors are what they do and not who they are.

Your child may be anxious or act angrily by screaming and yelling. This doesn't suggest that they are an angry child. It just shows that your child is someone who screams and yells when angry. Also, you can't say you have a disobedient child just because they failed to follow instructions.

Why is this distinction important, you may ask? No one wants their child to grow up feeling ashamed, damaged, or worried that they have a flawed character. You want your child to know that they are not their behaviors. You want them to feel loved and accepted despite their feelings and behaviors. If you want a child who will grow up with a positive image, you need to teach them that their behavior only defines what they do and not who they are.

Exercise: A Story of Emotion

This exercise aims to walk you through your *story of emotions*. For now, you will be learning skills that will help you change your response to situations, since having awareness is essential. However, as you continue reading this book and learning skills, your stories may change.

The first task is to recall a recent situation that stirred up negative emotions in you and write down a brief description of the situation.

The next task is to consider the questions below and write down your answers. While writing, notice where you've made changes.

<u>Your risk factors and vulnerabilities</u>:

Describe how you feel before the event occurs.

Your trigger:

What happened?

Your beliefs and thoughts:

What are your thoughts about what happened? What did you have to say after the event?

Responses and body sensations:

How exactly did your body feel?

Name your emotion:

What name can you use to describe what you felt?

<u>Your actions and behaviors:</u>

What was your reaction like as a result of how you felt? What response would've been better?

When you understand the story of your emotions, it puts you in a better place for self-awareness and changing how you interact with your child. But, of course, your child has their unique stories of emotions affecting how *they* feel or behave.

Life is already hard enough, and we aren't oblivious to that fact. But in this case, you aren't stuck or helpless in this tussle with your emotions. If you can do the work to implement the skills and strategies of DBT, your reactions to intense emotions will change, and you can make the same changes in your child.

The reason is simple. Regardless of genetics, DBT skills can influence the outcome of all anger and conflict, and they can alter the state of your relationship. Therefore, there is hope if you continue reading this book. What's in this book has changed the lives of many (for the better); it will change yours too.

CHAPTER 2:
EMOTION DYSREGULATION IN TEENS: A PHASE OR A PROBLEM?

Many parents think they are fully prepared for anything in their teenager's life because they've experienced both the "terrible twos" and the "extreme eights." However, parenting becomes a big deal when your child hits their teenage years. During this period, you can easily feel overwhelmed in managing the effects of puberty hormones, general teen angst, and social media influence.

Some teens even start acting in ways you can't recognize. In fact, many teenagers experience emotional dysregulation, a mental health symptom. Therefore, as parents, you need to know what to look for and how to seek help for your teen.

Parents experience the direct and experiential awareness of the unstable emotional lives of their children. Since you were once a teen and have experienced adolescence yourself, you should have an idea of what the emotional life of a teenager is like.

How exactly was your emotional life then? Was it rocky? Smooth? Did you have it all together or sometimes allow your emotions to get better of you?

I am guessing you experienced a combination of the above. Sometimes you experienced good days, while at other times it wasn't that great. But, regardless of their experience, most teens have experienced various kinds of days; even days when their emotions were all over the place and days that seemed like the worst time of their lives. And some days can also feel like the best they've ever had.

Now, I want you to look back and understand that the rollercoaster of emotions you've experienced in the past is part of your growth; it's your learning phase. I want you to empathize with your teen now and forgive them for their attitudes, impulsive behaviors, and moods. These expressions summarize how teenagers feel and look from the outside.

Of course, your teen is like that for a good reason. Their developing brains form from two directions simultaneously—top-down and bottom-up. The top part is the newest part of the brain, which generates logical thoughts, modulates emotions, regulates impulses, and weighs risk and reward. The bottom part, which is the oldest part of the brain, generates emotions and unconscious reactions.

To better understand whether emotional dysregulation is just a phase in a teen's life or if it is likely to pose a problem, let's start with discussing what emotional dysregulation means.

Understanding Emotional Dysregulation

The team at Rogers Behavioral Health suggests that people experience emotions differently, and some people experience emotions more intensely than others. People with intense emotions experience mood shifts with feelings that linger longer. However, when they find it hard to cope with their intense feelings, this will lead to emotional dysregulation.

But what is emotional dysregulation?

Emotional dysregulation is the inability to stay psychologically and emotionally balanced, resulting in counterproductive and maladaptive behavior. According to Clearview Women's Center for Mental Health, emotional dysregulation affects almost 3% of people in the United States. These people have difficulty managing their emotional responses, making them seem aggressive and conflict-driven.

Emotional dysregulation is more of a symptom than a disorder. Someone experiencing it can feel emotions more intensely than they should and might feel them for a longer period. As a result, they experience these emotions at inappropriate times and respond to them extremely. The common sign of it is extremely emotional instability and severe mood swings.

People who are more likely to experience emotional dysregulation are people with mood disorders and personality disorders. However, it's not limited to these people alone; it exists in other scenarios. For example, people with ADHD can experience emotional dysregulation even if it's not present all the time. Also, those with anxiety disorders or who are manic-depressive can experience emotional dysregulation.

As mentioned earlier, emotional dysregulation isn't so much a disorder as, rather, a symptom of something bigger.

One of the main causes of emotional dysregulation is childhood trauma, despite what the diagnosis usually suggests—anxiety, depression, PTSD, ADHD, and Schizoaffective Disorder. According to research, if you could properly trace it back, you'd find that there was trauma at some point in your teen's childhood.

But why and how does trauma cause emotional dysregulation? What does emotional dysregulation look like in teens? Can it become a problem? Is it okay to just live with it or must it be treated?

When a child experiences trauma, which can be as mild as minimal neglect or as severe as physical abuse, the brain gets affected. It's either that the brain's neural pathways don't form or they become damaged, preventing messages from getting to where they need to reach in the brain. As a result, the prefrontal cortex can be damaged by the trauma. The prefrontal cortex controls decision-making and emotional regulation, so imagine how it would feel if it's been damaged.

When the prefrontal cortex is underdeveloped or damaged, it becomes difficult to behave appropriately. Also, when the brain is in a survival mode much of the time, stress hormones and adrenaline will be released frequently into the body, causing different biological and neurological issues for teens.

Emotional dysregulation in teens may look like this:

It's important to know that puberty seems to exacerbate the signs of emotional dysregulation in teens. They struggle with managing their emotions because of the pool of hormones rushing through their bodies. They get so angry that they can ruin all the relationships they have.

Teens may experience extreme anger that doesn't come with a justifiable reason. They may cry excessively for a longer time and more intensely. They may become physically aggressive to other people and themselves too. They may experience bouts of impulsivity, resulting in harmful risk-taking such as suicidal ideation at an early age, and they may become overly fearful of what's in their future. Sometimes, there is a quick movement between the opposite ends of their emotional spectrum. For example, they may be elated one moment and feel depressed a few moments later. They experience extreme impulsivity and make poor choices without giving the options much thought.

Teens with emotional dysregulation struggle to integrate socially with their environment because their emotions run wild. Even when they try to integrate socially, they can't sustain it for long. They usually have trouble in school and get into fights easily.

Emotional dysregulation entails the extreme side of not being able to manage emotions.

While it's possible to live without treating emotional dysregulation, it can be challenging and threatening to some teenagers. According to a study published in the *Journal of Youth and Adolescence,* the inability to regulate emotions, and the trauma of experiencing them extremely, have caused an increase in suicide rates. Emotional dysregulation can completely disrupt your child's ability to live in a healthy way.

The treatment for this symptom varies; therapy and medications are usually the go-to options. However, using medication for teens can be complicated due to concerns for their developing brains. In addition, some medications can affect the brain, defeating the essence of the treatment.

Usually, teens with emotional dysregulation are treated with therapeutic interventions and environmental changes before medication is considered. These environmental changes could be in the form of modifications in the school environment, for example.

Note that no matter the treatment your teen is receiving to keep their emotions in check, this is a problem that should be closely monitored to ensure they are safe.

Don't be weary; there is hope for your child. There is hope for them to be in control of their emotions and not be consumed by them. However, it takes you as the parent to be helpful and intentional in this journey.

Exercise: Understanding Emotions

Why do you think you have emotions? Are your emotions good? Has there ever been a time when you cursed at your emotions? Perhaps, you wanted to get rid of them completely. Your emotions are useful for a couple of reasons, and you can change them since an emotion doesn't last forever. However, without understanding the functions of emotions, you can't expect to change them yourself. To further this understanding, answers to the questions below.

Think of a time you misread someone's emotions. What emotion were you able to read from them? Did the misinterpretation affect your interaction?

Do you remember a moment when your expression of emotion was misread? What kind of emotions did you feel? What emotions got misinterpreted? How did it feel to be misread by others?

Can you think of some situations where your emotions prompted you to take action before you could think about it?

Recall a moment when your emotion helped you overcome a challenge in your environment, making it easier to get something done — for example at home, in school, and in the community. Even though it's not a pleasant emotion, it helps you get something done.

What Causes Emotional Dysregulation?

For many years now, there has been ongoing research and debate surrounding the exact cause of emotional dysregulation. However, research indicates that teenagers who have experienced early trauma are more susceptible to developing maladaptive emotional patterns, also known as emotional dysregulation, than those who haven't.

The following are some childhood experiences that can lead to emotional dysregulation:

- Physical abuse
- Emotional abuse
- Sexual abuse and rape
- Physical neglect
- Emotional neglect
- Parental mental illness
- Parental alcohol and substance use
- Caregiver maltreatment
- Loss and grief (such as the death of a loved one)
- Exposure to domestic violence

Two things to note about teens with emotional dysregulation are 1) not every teen who experiences trauma in the early years will develop emotional dysregulation, and 2) the cause of emotional dysregulation isn't limited to what I've listed above. The trauma may result from your teen's environment, including trauma outside the home or neighborhood violence.

Some parents assume they are bad parents, and as a result, their kids have to deal with emotional dysregulation. If you are one of those parents, then you've assumed wrongly. Trauma is rooted in different origins, which may have no connection to parental behavior. However, if your teen is experiencing emotional dysregulation, you can assess yourself for any history of emotional dysregulation, mental illness, and alcohol abuse of your own.

We'll now discuss teenagers and what happens in their developing brains.

Teenagers and Their Developing Brains

During the developmental stage of adolescence, the bottom part of the brain outpaces the top part, and the old part becomes more powerful than the new one. On an individual level, the old part is referred to as old because it's one of the first parts to be developed. It's a limbic system associated with emotions and reward. It is where emotions like pain, pleasure, love, and fear emanate.

On an evolutionary level, the old part of the brain is referred to as that because, according to biology, the old part of the brain, in organisms with a complex brain, is the first to appear.

On the individual level, the new part of the brain is referred to as new because it's the prefrontal cortex, the last section to develop. This part of the brain is associated with complex logical thought, assesses and predicts outcomes according to information received, and prevents counterproductive behaviors. On an evolutionary level, the new part is referred to as that because, according to biology, the prefrontal cortex in an organism with a complex brain is one of the last structures to form.

No animal has a prefrontal cortex like humans. Therefore, when the oldest part of the brain becomes more powerful than the newest part, the resulting behavior may seem chaotic, uncontrolled, and irrational; the teen may act like a child.

When both the new and old parts of the brain start seeking dominance over each other, the teen's behavior may seem both logical and illogical within moments. This type of behavior is what we know as emotional dysregulation; examples of it include impulsivity, moodiness, and irrational behaviors.

In a typical teen behavior, while the emotions win some times, the prefrontal cortex wins other times. When diagnosed clinically, emotional dysregulation means that for different complex reasons, the brain develops regulatory functions that will lead to a mental illness (pathology).

According to evidence, emotional dysregulation in teenagers is associated with and is also a known risk factor for these mental health disorders:

- Anxiety disorders
- Eating disorders
- Depressive disorders
- Bipolar disorder
- Post-traumatic stress disorder (PTSD)
- Borderline personality disorder (BPD)
- Eating disorders
- Substance use disorder (SUD)
- Oppositional defiant disorder (ODD)
- Alcohol use disorder (AUD)
- Disruptive mood dysregulation disorder (DMDD)

Also, emotional dysregulation can be associated with as well as a risk factor for these maladaptive behaviors:

- Risky sexual behavior
- Non-suicidal self-injury (NSSI)
- Suicide attempts (SA)
- Suicidal ideation (SI)

The above behaviors and disorders are quite serious. Therefore, if a mental health specialist diagnoses your child with emotional dysregulation, there is a good chance the professional will suggest expert support and treatment at a psychiatric facility that specializes in handling adolescents with mental health issues.

Exercise: Knowing the Myths of Emotions

The aim is to introduce you to some myths about emotions and write a challenge that makes sense to you. A challenge will be provided – however, try to come up with another challenge for the myth or rewrite the one given.

Myth 1: *Allowing others to know that I feel bad is a sign of weakness.*

The challenge: Allowing others to know that you feel bad is a way to communicate your emotions.

Your challenge:

Myth **2:** *There is a particular way to feel in different situations.*

The challenge: We all respond differently to things, so there is no preferred or correct way to feel.

Your challenge:

Myth **3:** *My being emotional means that I am out of control.*

The challenge: My being emotional simply shows that I am only human.

Your challenge:

Myth 4: As the name suggests, negative feelings are bad and can destroy me.

The challenge: Negative feelings are natural responses that help me understand a situation better.

Your challenge:

Myth 5: I experience painful emotions due to my bad attitude.

The challenge: Painful emotions result from natural responses to a situation.

Your challenge:

Myth 6: Certain emotions are useless.

The challenge: All emotions indicate how I feel in certain situations. It doesn't mean they are useless as they all help me understand how I feel.

Your challenge:

Myth 7: If people don't approve of my feelings, I shouldn't be feeling that way.

The challenge: I have a right to feel how I do, regardless of what others think.

Your challenge:

Myth 8: *Others are the best judge of my feelings.*

The challenge: I should be the best judge of how I feel, as others can only guess.

Your challenge:

‑‑

‑‑

‑‑

‑‑

Myth 9: *My painful emotions should be ignored because they are unimportant.*

The challenge: My painful emotions can be warning signs indicating that a certain situation isn't good for me.

Your challenge:

‑‑

‑‑

‑‑

‑‑

Myth 10: *Extreme emotions will get me further than regulating my emotions.*

The challenge: Extreme emotions will only cause trouble for me and others. If emotions are extreme, emotional regulation should be helpful.

Your challenge:

Myth 11: *To be creative, I need intense and out-of-control emotions.*

The challenge: I can be in control of my emotions and still be creative.

Your challenge:

Myth 12: *Trying to change my emotions shows inauthenticity.*

The challenge: Change is inauthentic and is a regular part of life.

Your challenge:

Myth 13: *My emotions are a reflection of who I am.*

The challenge: My emotions can be partly, but not completely, who I am.

Your challenge:

Myth 14: *I can do whatever I feel like doing.*

The challenge: I can't do whatever I want because it might be ineffective.

Your challenge:

Myth 15: *Acting on my emotions is an indication that I am a free individual.*

The challenge: A truly free person has the ability to regulate emotions.

Your challenge:

Myth 16: I should always trust my emotions.

The challenge: Emotions can sometimes be trusted using logic.

Your challenge:

What Next?

Many teens struggle to manage their emotions to some extent. The rapid changes they experience in their physical appearance and the influx of hormones can confuse the brain in different scenarios. However, teens that have already experienced emotional dysregulation as a child will notice an extreme uptick in these difficulties when they hit puberty.

Some teens experiencing emotional dysregulation can be dangerous and self-destructive. They push people away and lash out due to anger, sometimes to the extent of ruining their relationships with friends and family members. They may feel depressed to the point that this impacts their ability to cope in school.

Some of the worst results of your teen's emotional dysregulation may come during their euphoric bouts of happiness. At these moments, it is easy to enter into extreme impulsivity and, as a result, engage in vices such as shoplifting, smoking, picking up a drug habit, driving erratically, and engaging in unprotected sexual activities. In other words, without proper management, emotional dysregulation can have fatal consequences for teens.

Naturally, as parents, we want to help our children as much as we can. But with emotional regulation, it becomes hard to know the best way to help. On the good side, mental health providers approve of DBT as working best for teens dealing with intense emotions. With it, you can track your teen's mood fluctuations. Also, you should write down everything you notice happening before, during, and after a mood shift, especially if it's extreme. That way, you can easily recognize possible triggers or what causes the mood swings.

You can try to validate your teen's emotions as much as possible during moments of extreme emotion. Since they feel no one understands them, the validation will help give your child possible relief. This has a calming effect on your child. Avoid lecturing, arguing, or trying to talk them out of their feelings during these times, because this will only aggravate the issue.

You can talk over the signs of emotional dysregulation you've noticed in your teen with your family doctor or any professional health care provider. A medical doctor will help determine if there is an underlying medical condition. If there is none, you will likely be referred to a psychologist or psychiatrist specializing in adolescents.

The clinical psychiatrist or psychologist will evaluate your teen to determine a possible diagnosis. A mental health provider will often recommend therapy and medication to help relieve the child's symptoms. Also, regular therapy can be suggested to help your teen work through their difficult emotions and learn to regulate and navigate them more effectively.

DBT is a form of therapy tailored for teens with emotional dysregulation. Dr. Marsha Linehan invented this therapy to help people manage disruptive behaviors or emotions when all approaches have failed.

Emotional dysregulation can feel overwhelming and seem scary. However, it is more common than people know. With the right approach, using DBT, your teen will learn how to work through their strong and overwhelming emotions and come out better in the end.

CHAPTER 3:
UNDERSTANDING YOUR CHILD'S EMOTIONS

Adolescence will probably not be complete if a teenager doesn't experience at least one episode of emotional outburst. Even you, a parent, went through extremely emotional moments while in your teenage years. This shows that occasional mood swings and emotional outbursts that occur sporadically are normal and are part of your teenager's growth.

Adolescence is a time of major transition, and this causes teenagers to experience a wide range of powerful and fluctuating emotions. Teenagers are still trying to find and accept their identity and the changes that come with it. You may notice that these emotional fluctuations often put them out of balance. Emotional outbursts are not considered important until they become extreme or constant and interfere with daily life. That may indicate a more serious mental health issue and should be looked into immediately.

Intense Emotions, Anger, and Anxiety in Adolescence: Causes and Contributing Factors

There are many reasons teenagers might experience frequent anger, anxiety, or other intense emotions. Teenagers experience emotional outbursts resulting from some seemingly unimportant things that could later prove to be a big deal. Sometimes, you might be able to discern the reason almost immediately. Other times, neither you nor your child can pinpoint why they react the way they do. These intense emotions could be a result of:

Heredity and family background

Do you know that some emotional disorders run in the family? If a family member, parent, or sibling suffers anxiety or depression, your teenager may likely inherit that. They may pick up your method of handling emotional tension too. For example, if you like venting out and creating tantrums when you are angry, your teenager may react in that same manner when experiencing the same emotions. According to research, young people whose parents fight and argue frequently or are overly involved in their children's lives have a high level of sadness and anxiety.

Toxic relationships

Relationships with toxic parents and peers can significantly impair a teenager's self-esteem, leading to emotional tension. Over-controlling, judgmental, frigid parenting, traumatizing social encounters, and emotional maltreatment increase emotional outbursts. You raise anger, induce anxiety, and contribute to sadness when you don't build a genuine relationship with your teen. The same thing applies to the kind of relationship your child has with their peers.

Medical conditions

Some diseases can produce symptoms related to emotional disorders or worsen their symptoms. For example, illnesses such as heart disease, lung issues, and thyroid problems may make your teen more likely to have emotional outbursts.

Certain medications used to treat these illnesses can increase or reduce anger, anxiety, and depression symptoms. This is why, when you or your teen stop or start taking some medications, you may experience intense emotions like anxiety or depression.

Change

Uncertainty bias has an impact on how a teenager deals with change. When a huge life shift occurs, the brain interprets that as a bad event. This can affect their decision-making process and make them feel more anxious and depressed. Teenagers who have experienced huge changes such as the birth of a new sibling, moving to a new house, or traveling to a different country are more likely to experience emotional outbursts. When teenagers feel uncomfortable in their surroundings, they are prone to experiencing a lot of tension and worry.

Environmental stress

Research studies have proven that environmental factors can also cause anxiety, depression, and anger in teenagers. However, these factors are mostly related to tense situations a teenager has witnessed or experienced. For example, childhood maltreatment, the death of a loved one, being bullied or attacked, and witnessing violence are common triggers for intense emotions.

Sleep deprivation

Lack of sleep can make a teen feel agitated and irritated. It can also affect their weight, memory, attention, and immunity. Your teen requires eight to ten hours of sleep per night to be mentally alert and emotionally balanced. Set a consistent bedtime for your teen and keep television and other gadgets out of their room to encourage healthier sleep. The light from these gadgets does not rest the mind. Instead, it decreases melatonin production and increases the activeness of the mind. They can try listening to music or audiobooks before going to bed instead.

Wrong eating or drinking habits

At this stage of their lives, teenagers are very likely to prefer junk or fast food to healthy food. Junk food could worsen your teen's mood and make them feel overwhelmed and tired. Anxiety disorder also occurs in conjunction with alcohol and substance abuse. Eating healthy food will do your teenager a lot of good. A healthy diet can help boost energy levels and mental sharpness and neutralize the teenager's mood. Make an effort to be a role model for your teen by doing more home cooking, eating more fruits and vegetables, and avoiding junk food and soda. These are all good ideas to improve the eating habits of your teen.

Warning Signs That Your Teen's Emotions Are out of Control

It's natural to have a surge of emotion from time to time. For example, if a teen is required to take an exam or make a significant decision, they may feel worried or nervous. However, intense emotions go beyond the teen's normal feelings of rage and grief. When it affects your teenager's capacity to function, it becomes distressing. In addition, they have little control over how they react in different situations. Therefore, it is advisable to address your teenager's outbursts in the early stages — before they become a habit or coping strategy.

You are probably lost and don't know the signs to look for that indicate your teen is out of control. Unfortunately, you aren't alone. It can be hard for caretakers or parents to know if their teens are just "being teenagers" or if it is something more severe. Some of the behaviors you see, such as mood swings, might be related to typical adolescent behavior and not necessarily point to a problem. Knowing when there are indicators of a more serious problem, on the other hand, can be very useful.

Some warning signs to show that your teen's emotions are out of control include:

Violent, disrespectful, or self-destructive behavior

If there have been episodes where your teenager slams the door in your face, stomps their feet in a fit of rage, or destroys nearby objects after being scolded, know that these are warning signs that teenagers with extreme emotional outbursts display. The teen often disrespects authority figures, throws unnecessary tantrums, and is not ready to listen to corrections. They might start damaging property, stealing, and engaging in fights. Arguments that never seem to end, domestic violence, getting into fights, and running into trouble with the law are warning signs that your teen is going beyond ordinary adolescent rebellion.

Use of hard drugs or alcohol

In a bid to relieve themselves of the emotional tension, some teens resort to the use of hard drugs and alcohol. When drinking or using drugs becomes a habit, especially if trouble at school or home follows from it, this could imply there's an underlying issue. Substance abuse is a risky coping mechanism. It causes the teen to lose sight of the main issue and focus instead on the immediate gratification they get from the drugs. Usage of heavy drugs is never a good sign.

Skipping school or withdrawing from social activities

When teenagers suddenly start to withdraw from participating in school or other social activities, their emotions may be out of control. The teenager might avoid meeting up with friends and dislike the company of others altogether. Going to school feels like stress, and they would rather be alone in bed all day long. A sudden change in their social circle could also be a concern, especially if the new friends support inappropriate behavior. The adolescent might begin to defy sensible rules and boundaries. Similarly, if your teen spends too much time alone, it could be a sign of trouble, so watch closely.

Persistent mood swings and engaging in early sexual activity

When mood swings become persistent and refuse to abate, there might be a problem. Sudden personality changes, declining grades, recurrent sadness, anxiety, or sleep difficulties could be signs of depression or other emotional health problems.

The adolescent may also be heard making sexually-explicit remarks or engaging in sexual activities. Requests to change their behavior will have little effect on them, and they will refuse to change despite the consequences.

When to Get Help for Your Child

If you're worried about your teenager's mental health, your family, friends, and partner may tell you to relax and wait until they grow out of it. This is sometimes sound advice, but that isn't always the case. There are occasions when waiting to get your child help for their mental health difficulties is simply not a good choice. The earlier a child receives treatment for emotional or behavioral issues, the easier it is to help them.

Emotional outbursts that occur regularly for six months or longer may indicate that your teen requires urgent assistance. These outbursts are usually more serious, including violent or disruptive conduct. You know you should get help for your teen when they start exhibiting:

Self-destructive behaviors

If your teen has attempted or threatened suicide or self-harm such as cutting or piercing themselves, you should seek urgent help. In addition, you should look out for the teenager's interaction with friends and classmates. This is because the teen might be injuring or threatening to injure others. Seek professional help if your child makes threats, fights, breaks things, injures themselves and others, or shows other aggressive behaviors.

Sit down with your child and try to talk to them the first time it happens. Try to figure out what's going on. Then, you'll need to teach your teen how to express their needs and the seriousness of their needs in a different, decent way.

Self-destructive acts could be their way of seeking attention. You could, however, teach them a more healthy way of demonstrating what they want. In this manner, whatever problems they have, you might be able to work together to solve them.

Sleep or eating disorders

If you notice a huge difference in your teen's sleeping or eating pattern, get help as soon as possible. An eating disorder often comes from using food to distract themselves or cope with an issue. The eating disorder should be addressed if a teen experiences rapid weight loss or gain, changes in shape, or feelings of dissatisfaction with body shape and size.

The teenager might also sleep in irregular patterns or lose sleep altogether. If there is a notable difference in your teen's sleep pattern, then this might be an indicator of an emotional issue. Seek the help of a professional. You could also encourage the teen to sleep by creating a bedtime routine to facilitate sleep. For example, have the teen decorate their room according to their preferences. They may control the amount of light and temperature in the room to help them sleep better. It may also be beneficial to pay greater attention to what they eat before bedtime.

Withdrawal from people and activities

If your teen suddenly begins to lose interest in the people or activities that used to thrill them, then you might need to seek help for them. Some emotional outbursts take the pleasure away from activities that were once enjoyable. Keep an eye out for your child's canceling plans or making up reasons to avoid doing things they used to enjoy.

Once you notice the continuous occurrence of these types of behaviors, an immediate measure is to request that your child go out with friends rather than lie in a dark room all day. Keep them occupied and engage them in fun activities to keep them around friends and family.

It is necessary to get help if your teenager's behavior is causing persistent problems at school or significantly disturbing your family life. You should also seek help if the teenager suddenly starts performing poorly in school and threatens to run away.

5 Strategies for Managing Your Child's Emotions

Parents are emotionally attached to their children. No parent can easily sit by and watch their teen wallow in self-pity and emotional derailment. It's difficult to watch your adolescent draw away from you, but patience and consistency are key in situations like these. Just because you have sought professional assistance, your work is not finished. You still have core roles to play as a parent. I can't promise that you won't get frustrated along the way. I can only guarantee that the following strategies will make things easier for you and your teen.

1. Give some time off

Do not follow your teen around, demanding apologies, while they are still enraged. This will simply prolong or exacerbate the fury. It may even result in a physical response. Instead, let your teen take a short time-out or ask for permission to leave the room for a moment of privacy. This should be done whenever they need to calm themselves down. Make it clear to your teenager that this is something they should do before they are tempted to misbehave.

Exercise: Assumptions Practice

Linehan gave several assumptions to guide the therapeutic work of DBT so it can be accepted as fact. These assumptions, including the ones developed by psychologist Alec Miller, are helpful for the parents of teens with intense emotions. They want you to accept these assumptions as an integral part of the DBT learning process. They include:

- There is no absolute truth
- The child is doing the best they can
- Your child wants to act differently and make things better
- Your child needs to try harder, do better, and be motivated to change

- Your child should learn new behaviors for important situations in their life
- Family members shouldn't assume the worst, but take things in a more well-meaning way

Examine these assumptions and think of how treating them as facts can change how you feel, think, and act. Then, answer the following questions.

Which assumption can help you the most, and why?

Which assumption challenges you the most, and why?

Recall a time when believing an assumption would have changed how you felt or what you did in the situation. Answering the questions below will help you clarify your thoughts:

Describe the details of the situation. For example, what was your child doing? How were they feeling?

What assumptions would you use? Check the list of assumptions.

Highlight a possible new response. For example, "I walked away and did not argue."

What do you think would be the result of the new response? For example — feeling calmer, yelling less, and experiencing no outbursts.

---

2. Validate and relate to your teen's feelings

Once your teen is calm, explain that there's nothing wrong with feeling angry. Still, there are unacceptable methods of expressing it. Some parents may unknowingly diminish a child's feelings, which is the wrong approach. Don't say things like "stay quiet" or "stop overreacting." If you say any of these things to your child, you're teaching them that their emotions are invalid. Instead, let them know that their feelings are valid even if they appear out of proportion at the moment.

That extra element of validation communicates to your child that everyone experiences such emotions at some point in their lives. At the same time, teach your youngster that emotions are transient, and the way they are feeling right now will last only a few minutes.

Even if you don't understand why your teen acts the way they do, letting them know you understand they're going through intense feelings may help. Let your teen understand that crying, feeling upset, and being irritated are not terrible things, nor are they marks of weakness for teenagers.

Exercise: Validation Practice

The steps below will help you practice validating your child. Read it repeatedly and always refer to it when facing a challenging situation or when you want to evaluate an interaction that you could've handled better. Practicing this exercise is important.

Step 1: Acting Wisely

You will stop, take a step back, observe, and think about the situation here.

- Take a moment before you respond
- Observe the situation you are in
- Identify the things you need to do to help slow down your reaction. For example—closing your eyes for a few seconds, taking a few deep breaths, and unclenching your fists
- Determine your goals
- Don't react emotionally—respond wisely

Step 2: Looking at your child with new eyes

This entails being aware of old patterns and developing new ways of thinking.

- Know that your child is doing the best they can under certain circumstances. Say this to yourself as a reminder.
- Think of what may be contributing to the present behavior.
- Help your child to think about what is going on. For example, is the present situation triggering difficult memories?

Step 3: Exploring what's getting in the way

Consider the possible circumstances impeding the validation of your child.

- What are the concerns or vulnerabilities you bring to the situation?
- Be aware of your feelings and thoughts concerning the situation.
- Has the event triggered old feelings or memories in you?
- Are you judging yourself or your child at this moment?

Step 4: Making a validating statement

It would help if you learned how to make statements that can help calm you and your child, showing your acceptance and understanding of them. It might not be easy at first, but with constant practice, you will find ways that work. Ensure your attempts are genuine.

3. Discuss healthy ways to relieve emotional tension

Many teenagers have outbursts because they don't know how to express themselves. When your teen is relaxed and not having a screaming fit, make some recommendations for better outlets. They need to understand that throwing items, cursing at others, or becoming physically aggressive are unacceptable reactions.

Let them know that if they do these things, there will be consequences.

Suggest healthy and decent ways to relieve their emotional tension. For example, practicing mindfulness, counting, listening to music, writing in a journal, painting, or engaging in a physical activity like walking or cleaning can help teenagers feel better.

Exercise: Being Mindful

Have them write their name slowly and notice how they hold the pen, rotating it into a comfortable position in their hand.

See how differently their name looks when they slow down to mindfully notice what they are doing.

Was it hard or easy for your child to do?

Notice that when they slow down their responses and focus more on their awareness, they can change their automatic response.

4. Identify mood boosters

Discuss with your teenager what they enjoy doing when they are happy. For example, they could enjoy playing a game, reading a comic book, or playing karaoke. Tell them that these activities are their "mood boosters," and they should write them down.

Encourage them to deal with their emotions by doing one of these activities when they are upset or sad.

Exercise: Boost Mood with the Six Senses

Vision: Let them go to their favorite place and take special note of the sights. For example, they can notice the people, colors, shapes, and sizes of things.

Smell: They should use their favorite body wash and aftershave, smell freshly brewed coffee, make popcorn or cookies, and take in the scent of fresh roses from the garden.

Hearing: They should listen to their favorite music repeatedly and pay attention to the sound coming from a musical instrument as well as the sounds of nature (thunder, rain, and birds chirping).

Taste: As they drink their favorite non-alcoholic beverage and eat their favorite foods, encourage them to do it mindfully.

Touch: They can try petting the cat or dog, brushing their hair, taking a long bath, hugging, changing into their most comfortable clothes, and putting a wet cloth on their forehead.

Movement: Suggest going for a walk together, exercising, dancing, and doing yoga.

5. Offer rewards

How you react to your teen's behavior immediately after it occurs determines whether or not the behavior will happen again. You can use rewards to encourage your teen to do the things you want. The best rewards are those that are given immediately after a behavior is exhibited. Both you and your teen will feel good when they act accordingly—you're happy because your teenager has accomplished something you like, and your teen is ecstatic as well since he is receiving something in return.

If you reward your teen with a special gift for pulling themselves together, they may learn to anticipate the gift that comes with controlling their emotions. While it's great to provide rewards, don't go overboard. You don't want your adolescent to learn that becoming upset is the easiest way to acquire your attention or get a gift from you.

Teenagers can be quite difficult to manage; it becomes even more difficult when they have emotional outbursts. Parents want the best for their teens, so they treat them in ways they think are best. You may be correct in some cases, but you may also be the source of your teen's outburst.

It's important to recognize that your child is growing and has outgrown the "baby" stage. Allow the child to choose what they want, but be present to guide and discipline them in a caring manner. Most times, forcing teenagers to do what you want them to do doesn't end well.

Teenagers may find it difficult to cope with emotions. Ensure that your teenager understands that you accept them for who they are. Be empathic and indicate that you genuinely care.

If your teen experiences anxiety or another emotional disorder that interferes with their normal activities, seek professional help. It is important to remember that your teen's emotional troubles aren't an indication that you've failed as a parent. Focus on your teen's current needs rather than assigning blame.

CHAPTER 4:
THE ROAD TO EFFECTIVE PARENTING

Parenting a teen with frequent emotional outbursts will unveil sides of you that you never knew existed. You might become as tensed up as your child and lose your cool at some point.

As parents, the way you react to your teen's emotional outbursts has a huge impact on them. Parenting a teen with frequent emotional outbursts can be difficult and overwhelming. It can sometimes force you to examine their actions and personal limits. Unfortunately, parents can unknowingly promote emotional outbursts in their children by becoming irritable and making offensive statements. This strategy has never been successful in controlling emotional outbursts.

The best way to control your child's outbursts is to try effective parenting. As you strive toward establishing a positive connection and raising a healthy, successful adult, it's critical to allow yourself to make errors and learn alongside your teen. Just keep in mind that the more effective you are as a parent, the "healthier" your adolescent will be.

What Is Effective Parenting?

Effective parenting goes beyond the regular type of parenting that simply provides food and shelter for the teen. It entails a deeper and more dedicated relationship with the child. Effective parenting is the ability of parents to interact and engage with their teens in encouraging them to learn and develop into responsible individuals. It is built on the principles of respect, discipline, boundaries, encouragement, and a variety of training and teaching possibilities. Effective parenting focuses on holding your teen accountable for their actions and helping them develop better problem-solving abilities.

Why Is Effective Parenting Good?

Effective parenting sets the tone for a child's personality, life choices, and overall behavior. It can impact their social, physical, and mental well-being. Teens who have a safe and healthy attachment to their parents are more likely to have happy and fulfilled relationships later in life.

Effective parenting teaches teens how to manage their emotions in stressful and tough situations. Socially, a child raised by parents who use effective parenting will be positive and confident. They raise children who have a better knowledge of the world and what is required of them as teenagers. They talk about the rules with their teens and make sure they understand what's expected of them. They also make certain there are consequences for their actions, regardless of how they feel.

Responding to Your Child's Feelings and Behaviors — Emotionally, Reasonably, and Wisely

The fury of a teenager can make parents uneasy. As a result, you could try to satisfy your teen by giving in to their demands or avoiding particular circumstances to alleviate their anger or unhappiness. Some parents also use intimidation or punishment to stop the rage. In other words, they become irritated and annoyed by their child's rage.

Your teen will, without a doubt, encounter situations that cause emotional outbursts. You can't stop the triggers from happening, but you can show your child the tools for understanding their feelings and teach them how to cope with these feelings healthily and reasonably. Your reaction to your teen's outburst will also influence whether or not your child reacts appropriately. Some parents react emotionally, some reasonably, and others wisely.

Reacting emotionally

Most likely, you're reacting emotionally if you parent primarily with irritation and wrath. However, if you have a short temper and react by yelling, this too is reacting emotionally to your teen's outbursts.

Reacting emotionally does more harm than good. When you are emotional, it is more difficult for you to solve problems, and making plans may seem impossible. You rant, complain, and yell, and the atmosphere becomes tense for both your teen and you. This has not solved any issue; it has simply made the situation worse.

Reacting reasonably

A parent who responds rationally most of the time may be unaware of how emotions affect others. This kind of parent rarely allows emotions to influence their decision-making. They feel calm and unaffected by the emotional outbursts that surround them. The parent will resolve most issues and feel highly confident in their ability to solve problems. On the other hand, they will be uncomfortable with emotions and unable to comprehend the feelings of teens or others. They may come off as too strict. Their teens may also dread having a relationship with them if they are sure to become greatly agitated when the problems have no immediate solutions. A father who reacts reasonably and calmly will frequently get annoyed with a mother who operates emotionally and vice versa.

Reacting wisely

Both of these reasonable and emotional parenting styles must be fused to make effective parenting possible. When a parent thinks emotionally, they are unlikely to think rationally or logically. Similarly, a rational parent will have trouble infusing emotions into their decisions or actions and may not recognize the emotions of others. When you react to situations wisely, you will handle your reactions intuitively, and there will be balance in them. You will be able to view the whole picture and use both emotion and logic in making your decision. A wise mind will make you feel more relaxed when making decisions. Reacting wisely will assist you in making the required adjustments to your reactions so that your child's emotional outbursts can be controlled too. If your child has strong emotions or frequently reacts emotionally, it is important for you to think and react as wisely as possible.

Key Features of Effective Parenting

Focusing on the positive rather than the negative is a foundational principle of effective parenting. This isn't to say you should disregard the negative; it just isn't your priority. It also doesn't mean you should become a liberal parent. Instead, the key features of effective parenting ensure that you can use your position as a parent to positively influence your teen's emotions and reactions. It also helps you react wisely to your teenager's emotional outbursts.

With the three positive parenting approaches listed below, you may effectively teach, train, and instruct your teen on controlling their emotions.

Making observations

Parental observation works best when parents and teenagers have a positive, open, and caring connection. Teens are more likely to talk to their parents if they believe they can trust them and will receive helpful counsel, and if parents are open and ready to listen and talk to them. Teenagers who are content with their parental ties are more likely to follow the rules.

It would help if you tracked how much money your kid spends and how long they stay online. Keep an eye on your teen's emotions and conduct at home and talk about any concerns you have. As often as possible, talk to your teen about how they feel and what they think. Know your teen's circle of friends. Talk to your child about their plans with friends and where they intend to go after school. These observations will assist you in getting to know your child better and detecting any early indicators of emotional disorders. Listening, asking questions, providing support and appreciation, and remaining involved in your child's life are ways to parent your teen effectively.

Encouraging, not praising

Encouragement and praise are not the same things. The difference between encouragement and praise is that encouragement recognizes effort, the process, and the celebration of progress. On the other hand, praise is a judgment and is about offering a teenager your approval for their activities. Praise instills a sense of reliance on the opinion of others, while encouragement emphasizes one's efforts and abilities.

Encouragement is more helpful than praise in boosting a child's self-esteem. Overuse of praise can reduce self-esteem in youngsters, making them more competitive and less cooperative.

Encouragement can be a very effective motivator. For example, instead of saying, "You're so calm now," say, "It's so nice that you've been able to work on your emotions." You encourage your child to keep behaving responsibly and positively by noticing and commenting on their responsible decisions and behaviors.

Discipline to teach, not to punish

Do not mistake appropriate parenting for the absence of unpleasant consequences. Effective parenting is not the same as allowing your child to do anything they want or as a "weak" attitude that allows your teen to get away with anything. There is still a place for discipline when parenting teens with emotional outbursts. The problem is that parents discipline their teens out of frustration. The punishment they give is meant to cause pain and not make the child understand that their reaction was wrong.

Your teen may occasionally act in ways that push your boundaries or violate the rules you've established. Outlining the consequences is an approach to dealing with this. If you can make the punishment correct the wrongdoing, your teen will be more likely to learn from the experience. For example, if your child breaks a plate in a fit of rage, a suitable punishment might be to have to replace it himself. This method seeks to assist your teen in understanding your point of view and learning that they must give and take to be successful. If they can benefit from doing the right thing, they should also face the repercussions of doing the wrong thing.

Parenting Strategies for a Child with Intense Emotions

1. Be a role model

Teens are wired to mimic, understand, and absorb the actions of others into their actions. Just like small children, they pay close attention to everything their parents do. Your teen will observe how you handle difficult situations.

How does your teenager perceive your dealings with their difficulties and coping mechanisms? Take time to walk the walk. Telling your child what you want them to do isn't enough; showing them is the best method of teaching them. Some of your emotional buttons may be pushed by your child's rage. If you're not conscious of your problems, you may react in ways that are harmful to your child. You could give in to their demands or yell back, but neither of these options will solve the problem. Take a deep breath if you find yourself experiencing strong emotions.

Be the person you want your teen to be, respect them, model positive conduct and attitudes, show empathy for their feelings, and your kid will follow suit. You can advise your teen on how to behave and give them various solutions. Still, if you're mishandling your own emotions (yelling, screaming, or doing something else that isn't positive), your conduct will take precedence over whatever you're advising them to do. You must try to control your outbursts. Then let your teen watch you work through it so they can learn from you.

Exercise: Use the PLEASE Skills

PL: Treat PhysicaL illnesses in your body. Take care of yourself and see a doctor when necessary. Always take the prescribed medication.

E: Balance your Eating by not eating too little or too much. Eat mindfully and avoid foods that make you emotional.

A: Avoid mood-altering substances, alcohol, and drugs.

S: Balance your Sleep. Ensure you get seven to nine hours of sleep every night; it will help to make you feel good. See a doctor if you have sleep disorders.

E: Exercise. Engage in a significant amount of exercise daily. You and your teen should build up to at least twenty minutes of exercise daily.

2. Find out why your teen is sad or upset

Helping your child cope with emotional outbursts will be a lot easier if you know the root cause of the problem. Try to figure out what is causing your adolescent's emotional outbursts. Is your teen stressed out as a result of a major family change? Are they being bullied in school? Do they feel inferior because their classmates have things that they lack? Does your adolescent need someone to listen to who doesn't pass judgment on them? Ask open-ended questions to get the teen to talk about why they're reacting in that way.

Asking questions will be successful only if you have a cordial relationship with your teen. If you and your teen are not on good terms, don't force it. Try to create a relationship by spending time together first. Let your teen open up at their own pace.

Exercise: Identifying What Helps Your Child Feel Better

When they are sad, they feel better when I…

When someone hurts their feelings, they feel better when I…

When they are mad, they feel better when I...

When they are upset, they feel better when I...

----

3. Problem-solve with your child

If there is a problem, suggesting solutions for your child can be beneficial, but your teen must be a part of the solution and feel like they "own" it. If your teenager believes the solution came from them, they will be more willing to try it. Problem-solving is also an important life skill that your child will improve by practicing. By devoting time and effort to improving your child's problem-solving abilities, you show that you respect their participation in life decisions.

Allowing your kid to figure out how to manage these situations, while assisting them, allows them to learn a difficult but crucial lesson about responsibility. It's critical to provide support and maintain empathy without taking on their troubles or bailing them out. You want your adolescent to understand that they can solve problems and build a sense of cause-and-effect relationships. By being supportive and there for them, you allow teens to understand that they are strong and capable. Ask about what tactics they think would be beneficial to them. With your help, they might be able to come up with some innovative ideas to help them cope with their emotions.

Exercise: Problem Solving to Change Emotions

This exercise involves selecting a promoting event that triggers a painful emotion, selecting an event that can be changed, and turning the event into a problem that needs solving.

Use the questions below to describe the event.

What is the problem? For example, describe the problem by prompting emotions and write down what makes the situation a problem.

Check the facts by looking back and identifying if there is an overreaction. What event triggered the emotion? What are the interpretations or assumptions about the event? Do the emotion and its intensity correlate with the assumption of the situation?

_____

_____

_____

_____

_____

Write down a realistic short-term goal of the problem-solving process. What has happened to show that progress has been made?

_____

_____

_____

_____

_____

It's time to brainstorm solutions. Write down as many of the solutions and coping strategies that come to mind. Don't evaluate them.

---

4. Show love and acceptance

Even though your teenager may feel enraged, unhappy, or anxious, they still require your love and attention. Your role might shift slightly because of their outbursts, but you are still their parent. Even if they claim to despise their parents, they still need the emotional support only parents can give. In addition, they need comfort and self-confidence to deal with peer pressure and other adolescent demands. Teens who lack confidence are more likely to succumb to peer pressure and struggle to uphold wholesome, ethical beliefs.

You're still in charge of keeping them safe; guiding and shaping the kind of adult they will become. They need to know you adore them no matter what and that you are always on their side. You need to show them love and reassure them constantly. Take them on trips, get them gifts, and encourage them. Teens still want your approval and support even when they are kicking and yelling, so try to constantly let them know that you love and accept them the way they are, even if you are dissatisfied or upset yourself.

Exercise: Paying Attention to Positive Events

It's natural for humans to pay more attention to the bad than the good. If you were given eight compliments and one criticism, you will likely ignore the compliments and focus on the criticism. If you've been focusing on the negative aspect of things, it's time to stop and refocus on the positive.

Start doing small positive activities with your teen, and don't let problems ruin the moment. Some of these activities include:

- Watching a movie together
- Having a satisfying, leisurely meal together
- Going for a walk
- Going on picnic dates
- Trying out a new hobby
- Visiting family and friends
- Visiting a zoo or local museum

Even though adding one or two positive activities won't change their lives, it will create happiness, which can add up and make a significant difference over time.

5. Establish boundaries and consequences

While correcting your teen with love, you also have to let them know that they cannot do certain things simply because they are in a fit of rage. At a time when both you and your teen are calm, make them understand that there are inappropriate ways of showing anger. If your teen, for example, destroys the door in a fit of rage, they will have to save money to get it fixed. They will lose some rights if they slam the door in your face.

Boundaries and restrictions are important now more than ever for teenagers; it would help if you established clear limitations and boundaries. Your ability to maintain a level of consistency gets you respect. Make it very clear what is and is not acceptable. It's preferable to have an adolescent who is temporarily enraged than a teen who does not respect you.

Exercise: Let Go of the Emotion, Not the Situation

Letting go of your emotions doesn't suggest letting go of the consequences or situation. It means you are weathering the emotions to become more effective. If you are having an argument with your child and you are angry, let go of the anger until it's dissipated, and then handle the situation more effectively.

You can practice deep breathing to help you maintain calm. To do this:

- Place one of your hands on your chest and the other hand on your abdomen.
- Start inhaling slowly and deeply. Make the air pass through your nose and into your abdomen.
- When you feel at ease with your breathing, inhale through the nose and exhale through the mouth.
- Continue with the slow deep breaths, which should be raising your lower abdomen.
- As you become more relaxed, focus on the feeling and sound of your breath.
- Continue this process for five minutes.

Practice this exercise whenever you feel tense. You can do it anywhere and in any position.

6. Stay connected

Staying engaged and actively listening to what is happening in your teen's life will allow you to more easily understand the triggers for their emotional outbursts. Sometimes the ideal moment for your child to share things with you is during informal, ordinary activities like driving your child somewhere, eating out, or watching TV together.

Parents usually spend more time talking to their teens than interacting with them. Practice paying attention to your children and truly listening to them. You'll be astonished at how much more connected you feel to your child. In addition, you'll probably learn a lot about what they've been thinking and experiencing.

When your adolescent is chatting with you, look at them. Paying attention to what they have to say gives your teenager the message that you value their input. Show that you're interested. Encourage your child to elaborate on what they've said and discuss their thoughts, feelings, expectations, or intentions. Listen without interrupting, judging, or correcting what they are saying. Your goal is to spend time with your child, not to offer advice or assistance until they specifically need it.

Exercise: Describing Your Child in Non-Evaluative Terms

This exercise encourages parents to use descriptive rather than judgmental language with their teens. You can do this by picturing your teenager standing in front of you, then writing down your answers to the following questions.

How does your child look? For example, what's the color of their hair and eyes, and how tall are they? NOTE: Don't use words like skinny or fat because these can be perceived in evaluative ways.

_____

_____

_____

_____

_____

What does your child enjoy doing? What are their hobbies? What's their favorite food? What's their favorite sport?

_____

_____

_____

_____

_____

_____

How does your child spend their day? What grade are they in school? What's their favorite subject? Do they enjoy sports? What sports team are they rooting for?

Does your child have a talent for playing a musical instrument or performing?

You can use many more ways to describe your child than you normally think about. The point is to focus on your child's other qualities rather than just on their emotional intensity. This exercise should help you see your child with new eyes and in new ways.

Finally, managing the emotions of teenagers can be daunting because they are still developing an identity of their own. Effective parenting and reacting wisely will make the job a lot easier. If you take advantage of casual talks during the day, you and your teen will start feeling closer. Think of ways to effectively communicate with your teen and teach them new, acceptable behaviors. Every small conversation is an opportunity to listen to your teen and form bonds with them. Being kind to your teen also helps to foster a cordial relationship. Start saying "please," giving hugs, knocking before entering their bedroom, and cooking their favorite meals. You may have to put your emotions aside once more and think critically.

These activities create a cheerful atmosphere. Even if you don't feel like it, make an effort to be kind to your teen. This sets a good example for your child and demonstrates the importance of spending time together. Teenagers are different—each has their own weaknesses, strengths, and peculiarities. Seek professional help if the strategies you've tried don't give relief, and keep trying. Also, remember that this phase will pass.

FINAL WORDS

You've reached the end of this amazing journey. I must commend you for staying with me to the finish.

No doubt about it, the teenage years can be quite challenging for any parent. Teenagers may behave recklessly, act notoriously moody, and be unpredictable, making parenting difficult. It's even more difficult for parents with teens who are experiencing emotional dysregulation.

While many teens troubled by anxiety and anger issues require professional treatment to feel better, there are ways parents can help them manage their issues. I hope this book has delivered on its promise of providing effective strategies for managing your teen's intense emotions.

With the right support and guidance, you can help your teen learn new ways to manage their feelings and find more happiness and success in life.

A Kind Request

I hope you enjoyed reading! Please share your thoughts about the book by **leaving an Amazon review**.

Your review doesn't have to be elaborate. Even if it's only a sentence or two (although the longer the better!), It will be very helpful.

Please go to the below URL to post your review now.

www.thementorbucket.com/review-dbt-set

Thank you,

The Mentor Bucket

NEXT READ

LIFE SKILLS
FOR TEENS WORKBOOK

35+ Essentials for Winning in the Real World

(How to Cook, Manage Money, Drive a Car, and Develop Manners, Social Skills, and More)

Go to the below URL
for more details.

www.thementorbucket.com/life-skills-teens

A FREE GIFT TO OUR READERS

For being our valued reader, we wanted to offer you a FREE gift.

What You'll Get:

✓ **11 Essential Life Skills** *Every Teen Need to Learn Before Leaving Home*

✓ *How to* **Be A Calm Parent** *Even When Your Teens Drive You Crazy*

✓ *15 Tips to* **Build Self-Esteem and Confidence** *in Teen Boys & Girls*

Download your FREE gift here.

www.thementorbucket.com/gift-dbt-set

DOWNLOADABLE WORKSHEETS

Go to the below URLs to download all worksheets (in pdf format) given in the book.

Worksheets of book - 1:

www.thementorbucket.com/dbt-ws1.pdf

Worksheets of book - 2:

www.thementorbucket.com/dbt-ws2.pdf

RECOMMENDED BOOKS

Go to the below URL and check
our recommended books.

www.thementorbucket.com/resources